The International Library of Sociology

SIGMUND FREUD
AN INTRODUCTION

Founded by KARL MANNHEIM

The International Library of Sociology

SOCIOLOGY OF BEHAVIOUR AND PSYCHOLOGY
In 18 Volumes

I	The Development of Conscience	*Stephenson*
II	Disaster	*Wolfenstein*
	(The above title is not available through Routledge in North America)	
III	The Framework of Human Behaviour	*Blackburn*
IV	Frustration and Aggression	*Dollard, Miller et al*
	(The above title is not available through Routledge in North America)	
V	Handbook of Social Psychology	*Young*
	(The above title is not available through Routledge in North America)	
VI	Human Behaviour and Social Processes	*Rose*
	(The above title is not available through Routledge in North America)	
VII	The Human Group	*Homans*
	(The above title is not available through Routledge in North America)	
VIII	Learning Through Group Experience	*Ottaway*
IX	Personality and Problems of Adjustment	*Young*
	(The above title is not available through Routledge in North America)	
X	Psychology and the Social Pattern	*Blackburn*
XI	The Sane Society	*Fromm*
XII	Sigmund Freud – An Introduction	*Holitscher*
XIII	Social Learning and Imitation	*Miller and Dollard*
XIV	Society and Nature	*Kelsen*
	(The above title is not available through Routledge in North America)	
XV	Solitude and Privacy	*Halmos*
XVI	The Study of Groups	*Klein*
XVII	Theory of Collective Behaviour	*Smelser*
	(The above title is not available through Routledge in North America)	
XVIII	Towards a Measure of Man	*Halmos*

SIGMUND FREUD
AN INTRODUCTION

A Presentation of his Theory, and a Discussion of the Relationship between Psycho-analysis and Sociology

by

WALTER HOLLITSCHER

First published in 1947 by
Routledge, Trench, Trubner and Co., Ltd

Reprinted in 1998, 2001, 2002
by Routledge
2 Park Square, Milton Park, Abingdon, Oxon, OX14 4RN
or
270 Madison Avenue, New York, NY 10016

First issued in paperback 2010

Routledge is an imprint of the Taylor & Francis Group

British Library Cataloguing in Publication Data
A CIP catalogue record for this book
is available from the British Library

Sigmund Freud: An Introduction
ISBN 978-0-415-17792-4 (hbk)
ISBN 978-0-415-60587-8 (pbk)
The Sociology of Behaviour and Psychology: 18 Volumes
ISBN 978-0-415-17834-1
The International Library of Sociology: 274 Volumes
ISBN 978-0-415-17838-9

Publisher's Note

The publisher has gone to great lengths to ensure the quality of this reprint but points out that some imperfections in the original may be apparent

TABLE OF CONTENTS

PREFACE

The aim of this book is to present the sociologist with the main psychological ideas of Freud and to stimulate discussion on the possibilities of co-operation between psycho-analysis and sociology.

The first purpose is served by a statement of Freud's views on important parts of psycho-analytic theory. This statement is closely based on a *montage* of extracts from Freud's own writings. Considerations of copyright prevent the textual reproduction of lengthy quotations, but in all essential points an attempt has been made to stick closely to Freud's own sequences of thought and his formulations. In footnotes the reader will find indicated the passages in Freud's works which have been paraphrased. In this part of the book I have tried to make myself as little seen and heard as possible and to leave the stage entirely to Freud. If the reader should find here and there some abruptness of transition from one section to the next, he may find compensation in the fact that what he is being offered is pure Freud and not somebody else's interpretation of him. I have avoided any intrusion of my own thoughts and resisted all temptations to modify what he actually said.

In the service of the second purpose, to stimulate co-operation between psycho-analysis and sociology, I have written an introductory essay and a postscript in which I present my own views on the prospects and difficulties of such a co-operation. In addition to this, in the second part of the Bibliographical Guide, titles of books and articles are collected which either show how psycho-analysis has hitherto been applied to sociology or discuss the relationship between psychology and sociology in more general terms. I have to thank very warmly Dr. E. Kris and Dr. Leites, of New York, for furnishing me with a number of titles concerning the relationship of psycho-analysis to sociology.

I wish to thank Professor Karl Mannheim, the editor of this series, not only for the stimulation which this book owes to his concern to establish co-operation between branches of knowledge which have so far existed in watertight compartments, but also for the contribution of many valuable items to the last part of the Bibliography.

I am very grateful to Mr. Fritz Friedmann for assisting me

with corrections, and to my friend, Mr. Vivian Ogilvie, who not only translated my Introduction and Postscript but also took an essential part in the formulation of the middle part of this book, which sets out Freud's doctrine.

Finally I wish to express my gratitude to the Hogarth Press and the Institute of Psycho-Analysis, London, on whose published translations this statement of Freud's views is based. I only hope that this book will stimulate the reader to make himself acquainted with the full range of Freud's imperishable achievement.

WALTER HOLLITSCHER.

August, 1946.

INTRODUCTION

CONCERNING THE RELATIONSHIP BETWEEN PSYCHO-ANALYSIS AND SOCIOLOGY

It is obvious that we cannot expect to gain insight into the feelings, desires, thoughts, actions, and achievements of a fellow human being, unless we have considerable knowledge of his social surroundings: his family background, and the class to which it belongs, his school, his work, and all the various other social institutions that influence him from the cradle to the grave. It is equally true, on the other hand, that any attempt to understand the origin and development of social institutions such as these raises the question: what were the psychological characteristics of the people who produced those institutions?

The connection between the psychological and social sciences appears to be of such an intimate nature that one is surprised that they have not long ago been merged into a single discipline, presenting the individual against the historical background of his age and historical events as psychologically explicable products of human activity.

But in fact this is not the actual state of affairs at all. Different schools of psychology explain human behaviour in such extremely different ways that the puzzled sociologist faces a difficult choice. And when the psychologist asks for the historical background he requires, he is offered a no less generous variety of interpretations, ranging through all shades from the religious to the materialistic conception of history.

The choice to be made is not simply a matter of taste. It is a question of scientific validity. Psychologists, sociologists, and historians must all alike accept the obligation to prove the correctness of their theses. Fortunately the criteria of truth they have to employ in so doing are not so different as some philosophers would have us believe.

The author of this book is of the opinion that the sociologist, in so far as he takes an interest in the psychological mechanisms of the human beings of whom he treats, cannot dispense with a thorough knowledge of psycho-analytic psychology. This school of psychology centred its investigations on the really key questions of psychological behaviour (instead of on the classification of smells or the ability to memorize meaningless sequences of syllables, fascinating though such problems may be), without at the same time committing the error of viewing man detached from his social surroundings. In short it seems to me the best that psychology has at present to offer to the sociologist. It will be my task to prove this.

The psychologist should, however, be chary of promises in his dealings with sociologists. There is current, it seems to me, an elementary misunderstanding, according to which psychology usurps—or ought to usurp—the function of the historian and to "explain" historical events by means of psychological short-cuts. The argument runs something like this. Human actions are determined by conscious and (if the analysts are right) unconscious motives. Further, it can hardly be denied nowadays that history is made by man, that historical events are the consequences of human activity. From this the "conclusion" is drawn that in respect of every historical event it should be possible to find in the persons concerned conscious or unconscious motives aiming at the production of this event. I do not know whether this is seriously considered to be a logical conclusion. It would be humiliating to think so. However that may be, the hope of clarifying the division of labour between psychologists and sociologists makes it appear justifiable to look a little further into this fallacy. By doing so we may hope to remove some fundamental misunderstandings.

Let us start with a very simple example. Suppose we come to a river and find that the bridge which starts at one bank does not lead to the other: it has broken down in the middle. Now we know that bridges are made by men. But should we conclude therefore that somebody, either consciously or unconsciously, set out to construct not a serviceable but an unserviceable bridge?

Obviously there is such a thing as the miscarriage of an intention, be that intention conscious or unconscious. This alone would forbid us to draw from an historical event a direct conclusion regarding the intentions of the actors.

Now let us consider a less trivial case. There is a rumour that a bank is in difficulty. In order to save their investments the creditors make a "run" on the bank, as a consequence of which, instead of saving their money, they precipitate their loss or even become its cause. Would it now be right to conclude that those people *wanted* to lose their money? Even if one among them, who was familiar with the mechanism of "runs", was led by conscious or unconscious self-destructive motives, so that he in fact succeeded in achieving the goal of his urge, the motive of the mass of creditors would still be the conscious one of saving their money. And unhappily the result was precisely the opposite. (Incidentally this is what often happens when people interfere with institutions whose mechanism they do not grasp—although those institutions themselves are naturally man-made.) But no self-respecting psychologist would postulate a wave of self-destructiveness merely because the behaviour of these masses brought about the crash of their bank.

This instance demonstrates one thing plainly enough: in history, what the actors desire to bring about, either consciously or unconsciously, does not always happen. Frequently their interests and intentions run contrary to each other. If a psychologist attempted to explain the conclusion of a wages agreement, he would consider the intentions of the employer or company regarding the rate of wages, and those of the workmen or their trade union. Further he would have to take into consideration any changes that might have occurred during the period of the wages conflict in the market in which the employer intended to offer his carefully calculated commodities, as well as any changes that might have taken place in the labour market in which the workers negotiate the price of their labour. The employer may possess psychological peculiarities caused by childhood experiences which make him particularly strong-minded or particularly soft-hearted. He may be a Tory or a Liberal. The trade union leader may harbour conscious or unconscious hatred towards the employer. He may wish to show his usefulness as a mediator (or, dazzled by Hollywood, as a future son-in-law). It would be hopeless to try to construct a sort of psychological parallelogram of forces from these factors, whose direction and strength are in part unknown, with the idea of thus foreseeing the result brought about in these particular historical circumstances by the consciously or unconsciously motivated actions of the persons concerned.[1] When sociologists try to foresee the trend of the

[1] Cf. Letter written by Engels to Joseph Bloch :—

London,
21st September, 1890.

". . . history makes itself in such a way that the final result always arises from conflicts between many individual wills, of which each again has been made what it is by a host of particular conditions of life. Thus there are innumerable intersecting forces, an infinite series of parallelograms of forces which give rise to one resultant—the historical event. This again may itself be viewed as the product of a power which, taken as a whole, works *unconsciously* and without volition. For what each individual wills is obstructed by everyone else, and what emerges is something that no one willed."

wages curve, they do not usually engage in psychological research into motives. They avail themselves of their knowledge that correlations exist between ascertainable facts (of a non-psychological nature) and the fact they are seeking to ascertain, and they base their predictions on these correlations which they call sociological or economic laws. We psychologists follow their exertions with admiring interest.

It will by now be clear what the misunderstanding is which these remarks are meant to obviate. Psychology, or in our case psycho-analysis, does not undertake to give a direct explanation of historical events and developments by means of those feelings, desires, thoughts, and springs of actions which it has discovered in men in the course of research. This would be a hopeless endeavour in our society, full of conflicts as it is, where the relations between the different classes are exceedingly indirect. Its method is nevertheless capable of throwing light on the psychological mechanisms with which men react to the stimuli of the world inside them and the world around them. By means of these reactions they reproduce in each generation the social conditions they were born to and sometimes even reshape them. No one will deny that in order to explain the behaviour of individuals a knowledge of the particular psychological mechanisms operating within them is indispensable. On the other hand, that the facts which occupy the historian and sociologist—to put it crudely, human institutions and their development—cannot be psychologically explained as consequences of individual intentions, our previous remarks tried to suggest. (We shall have to go into the matter more thoroughly in the concluding chapter.)

There is, however, an extensive intermediate field whose characteristic is that within it sociologists make ample use of psychological concepts and theories, while psychologists do the same with those of sociology. The subject-matter of this field is the theory of the behaviour of differentiated human groups or, in a certain sense, the differentiating theory of group behaviour. This commonly goes under the name of social psychology.

The topics which fall within this field are legion. In describing e.g. the rôle of the leader in relation to the members of his party, the rôle of parents and teachers in the education of the young, the attitude of the white workers to the black or the white student to his negro colleague, the attitudes of the criminal, the revolutionary and the petit-bourgeois to the police, of the newspaper reader to the editor, of the picturegoer to the ideology of the producer, who could avoid making extensive use of historical-sociological as well as psychological concepts and theories? It is a matter of frequent complaint that in doing so an author uses the latest theory in his own subject and the last theory but one (if not two) in the other subject, and is apt to combine well-informed perspicacity with something like naïve gullibility. In all these problems our concern is not only *what* happens in society and under what economic, social, and national circumstances, but, so to speak, *how* it happens, what psychologically takes place in the actors. To know this is necessary if we want thoroughly to understand these social processes, as well as useful if we intend to change them by direct intervention.

One word more to define more precisely the character of this special field. Such a combined sociological-psychological investigation is called for when the individuals forming a sociologically defined group display common psychological peculiarities which are of social relevance.

The " white workers of New Orleans " are, for example, such a sociologically defined group; they are people who all occupy a similar position in the process of production. If they also have common psychological characteristics (however they may have come by them), as a consequence of which they display an approximately homogenous attitude towards the equally sociologically defined group of negro workers, then the conditions are fulfilled which make this particular complex of problems a proper subject of study for a differentiating social psychology.

The reverse may also happen: a psychologically defined group may, by virtue of what its members have in common, constitute a social group, which would then come to be marked by further psychological peculiarities.

Thus, for instance, homosexuals may, because of their psychological peculiarity, form circles for the sake of companionship within a social group. The members of these circles now develop further psychological peculiarities as a group, for example, a common submissiveness for fear of the threat of exposure. (A phenomenon well known and feared inside political parties.)

When we described topics of this kind as comprising a special intermediate field, we did not intend to define the extent of this field. I believe it to be extensive, and by no means sharply separated from the adjoining fields of psychology on the one side and sociology (and history) on the other. The borderline is blurred by the fact that almost every sociological treatise contains remarks on psychological mechanisms, and vice versa. Both sets of remarks frequently take the form of unjustified generalizations—pronouncements about groups that are too extensive and not sufficiently differentiated. The sociologist, for example, may make general pronouncements about the state of mind of "*the* German youth" and the psychologist about "*the* causes of anti-semitism". Social psychology, therefore, is usually concerned with *differentiated* groups, because no statement can be made about general and undifferentiated ones, which is both true and worth making.

We have now, I hope, removed some obstacles. One could hardly get very far with a social-psychological work if one were not aware of them.

Our subject proper starts with a preliminary enumeration of those psychological mechanisms, a knowledge of which we declared to be indispensable for the social psychologist.

It is useful to realize that most books treating of our subject employ a terminology almost all of which is to be found in everyday speech and may well be called pre-scientific. It seems to me that it is frequently unscientific as well. For the realm of everyday psychological impressions and judgments is often one of illusions which we choose to have about ourselves and our fellow beings. It constitutes an attempt to catch non-existent fish with blunt hooks. We speak of "thoughts" as though they were a sort of cinema show taking place in strict privacy before our mind's eye. We speak of people who "love" and "hate", "admire" and "despise", "judge" and "sympathize", "educate" and "obey", and we imagine that we have said something clear and correct. In reality, once we try to express ourselves a little more clearly, we meet as a rule with the most unexpected difficulties. And if we at last succeed in giving an exact description of what we meant, it often turns that there is no such thing at all! One might almost believe that the angel who drove the first psychologist into the realm of reality must have proclaimed: "By their terminology ye shall know them."

We have already referred to psychological mechanisms, by which we meant those regularities of behaviour which psychologists have discovered in the course of their researches.

Now, Freud discovered that a knowledge of people's conscious or easily remembered feelings, thoughts, desires, etc., is not sufficient to explain their behaviour. The psychologist needs in addition to know a number of data of which the individual is unconscious, but which by means of psychological mechanisms—unconscious mechanisms—decisively influence his behaviour, both in general and in detail.

These unconscious motives of human behaviour are of widely different origin. They come from sources which are known to the biologist (or should be known to him—here Freud had many gaps to fill): that is, they are of an instinctual character. They come, too, from sources with which the sociologist should be familiar: from deposits precipitated in the mind of the individual by the human, the social milieu, without his being aware of it. What we call "conscience" in everyday language is the shunting-yard of these determinants of our behaviour.

This "unconscious" is not a rare animal which Freud discovered in the jungles of the soul, as Sir Harry Johnston discovered the okapi in the primeval forest. It is not a question of a single unknown fact which had hitherto eluded the attention of scientists, but of undiscovered laws, without a knowledge of which it is impossible to attempt to predict the peculiar features of human behaviour. It is as though someone tried to predict the refraction undergone by rays passing through a system of lenses by their appearance, describing them with epithets like "beautiful", "glittering", "sparkling", etc., and then discovered suddenly that what matters is index of refraction and radius of curvature. That is where the theory of lens systems begins; what he practised before belongs rather to the province of play or magic than of science.

Many of these psychological mechanisms are of the greatest interest to the sociologist. There is, for instance, the mechanism of *identification*, by means of which we imitate our models; that of *super-ego formation*, by which we internalize the social demands of our milieu; that of *transference*, by which we repeat attitudes acquired in a certain situation, in other situations which may be quite different; that of *sublimation*, by which impulses directed towards goals which society bans, are deflected towards goals which are likely to meet with indifference or approval; that of *rationalization*, by which without indulging in conscious hypocrisy we substitute for our actual motives or many of our thoughts, others which we can bear more easily. And there are many others.

In the following pages I shall endeavour to prove that all this is not an inventory of slogans, but an enumeration of tool-concepts of psychological scientific practice. We shall also show there that the mechanisms which these concepts denote are of the greatest social-psychological relevance.

For, if we want to understand how people fit into their social milieu and adapt themselves to it, we must know the nature of their reaction to internal and external stimuli. Now the way in which a person reacts is determined by his instinctual equipment. Like all living beings he strives to satisfy his instinctive desires in the environment in which he finds himself. What the objects of these desires are, however, depends not only on his biological nature, but also on the " conditioning " to which he has been subject—the vicissitudes that determine the relative strength of the various impulses in any particular individual. It will be appreciated why the social psychologist needs both the biological knowledge of man's instinctual equipment, and this psychological and sociological knowledge of the influences of the outer world, which—within the biologically given frame of possible instinctual goals—determine the actual, historical choice of a particular instinctual goal.

Thus, our exposition of psycho-analytical theory " for sociologists " must not omit the theory of instincts.

After studying the different psychological mechanisms mentioned above, we shall be in a better position to understand how the conscious and unconscious reactions of individuals and groups lead to the individual and group behaviour which interests the sociologist.

Those who know the extent of Freud's lifework and of the literature of psycho-analysis may well ask themselves how all this can be coherently described in a small book. That would indeed be an impossible task. Also, an undesirable one, for why should we try to deceive our readers into believing that they can do without the study of Freud's works? Freud was a most economical writer, a writer of classical stature, who states what he has to tell his readers in just as many words as are required to make himself understood without ambiguity.

The purpose of the next part of this book is to set out those conceptions and theories of Freud which the sociologist cannot dispense with if he is interested in what is going on inside the people of whose social behaviour he treats.

THE UNCONSCIOUS [1]

Suppose I experience some perfectly ordinary mental event. For example, I think of my parents' house or I desire to buy a gramophone or I feel angry at having lost my umbrella. The thought or desire or whatever it may be is present to my consciousness : I am aware of it. A moment later it has gone : it is no longer before my consciousness : I am not aware of it any more. Then, after an interval, it may come back again, just as it was before. No fresh perception through the senses has occurred in the meantime to cause its reappearance. We say that it has come back from memory.

This fact is so familiar that it may seem to call for no explanation. Yet a moment's reflection leaves one asking : what happened in the interval ? The account we normally give of this matter is that, somehow or other, the thought or desire or emotion has been in my mind all the time, though it was not present to my consciousness. It was "latent". In what form it continued to exist, we do not commonly attempt to imagine.

Philosophical Objections

The whole supposition of the persistence of mental elements while we are not aware of them has been criticized on philosophical grounds. The objection is made that the latent thought cannot be said to have existed as anything *psychical* at all. It could only have existed as a *physical* disposition for the same psychical phenomenon to recur. To this objection we may make at least three replies. First, it implies a theory that runs far beyond the domain of psychology proper. Secondly, by assuming the terms "conscious" and "mental" to be synonymous, it simply begs the question. And, thirdly, the objectors are quite out of order in denying to psychology the right to account for its most common facts, such as memory, by its own means.

Obviously the first step to be taken is to clarify our use of the terms "conscious" and "unconscious". Freud proposes that to start with we should only call a thought or other mental

[1] Coll. Pap., vol. iv, pp. 21–29 [A Note on the Unconscious in Psycho-Analysis].
Coll. Pap., vol. iv, pp. 101 ff. [The Unconscious].
The Ego and the Id, pp. 14 ff.
Introductory Lectures, pp. 240 f., 248 ff.
For abbreviations of titles see the Bibliography.

element "conscious" if and when it is present to the consciousness, i.e. if I am aware of it. If it is latent, if it exists in my mind but I am not at the moment aware of it, it should be called "unconscious".

But if I am not aware of it, how can I know it exists? From the nature of the case, the evidence can only be indirect. I can only infer it from indirect signs, from circumstantial evidence. Memory is the example that lies readiest to hand. You mention the Norman Conquest. The date 1066 comes to my mind. Until you spoke the date was not present to my consciousness: I was not thinking of it, as we say. Yet I had been aware of it at times before, and now I am aware of it again. The testimony of such everyday experiences makes us ready to admit that the date has remained in my mind all the time, "latent."

How we Ascribe Mental Life to Other Persons

There is nothing very odd about postulating the existence of mental elements of which we are not directly aware. It is what we always do where other people are concerned. For the fact is that the only states of mind of which I can be directly aware are my own. As far as other people are concerned, I can only attribute to them the possession of states of mind—or indeed of consciousness—by inference and analogy. I see them carrying out actions, I hear them speak, and the only conclusion I can draw to render their behaviour intelligible is that they are made in the same way as I am, that they are conscious and have states of mind.

Because of these facts, the methods of acquiring psychological data have been traditionally given as two: by introspection and by observation.

We all take the identity of other human beings with ourselves for granted. But it is not a direct awareness. It is an inference. The inference is spontaneous and universal. In fact, men have by no means restricted it to human beings. It has often been extended to animals. It has even been extended to plants, inanimate objects, the world at large. Among primitive peoples and small children the gulf between the ego and other objects was, or is, not very great. With the advance of knowledge the gulf has widened and to-day we refuse to attribute consciousness to sticks and stones and even plants; we are doubtful about attributing it to animals. Only in the case of our fellow men has the assumption of consciousness survived criticism. But—let it be repeated—even in this universally accepted instance, the attribution of consciousness is an inference; it does not possess the direct certainty that we have of our own consciousness.

What psycho-analysis asks us to do is to apply this same method of inference to ourselves, however little we may be inclined to do so. What does this amount to? It amounts to looking at our own actions in the same way as we look at those of another person. If the actions of another person seem at first sight difficult to account for, we are not content to write them off as arbitrary, mysterious, and inexplicable. We try to account for them. We try to discover what caused them. We assume, that is to say, that the other person's mental life forms a system of cause and effect; that his thoughts, desires, feelings, etc., are conditioned and subject to a certain regularity. We believe that identifiable mechanisms are at work. So we try to fit his, at first sight inexplicable, action into the context of his total mental life and account for it by what we believe we know of the principles which operate in it. We all do this and we are reasonably good at it. But when we turn to ourselves and notice actions or other manifestations which we are unable to link up with the rest of our mental life, we hesitate to follow the same procedure. We find it difficult to acknowledge that our own actions, thoughts, desires, emotions, are conditioned. The idea of tracing their causes is repugnant to us. There is a peculiar obstacle in the way of our applying to ourselves the methods of investigation that we apply to others. And this stands between us and a true knowledge of ourselves.

But supposing I overcome my reluctance and apply the same method of inference to myself, what does it yield? According to Freud it does not lead at once to the discovery of an unconscious. The conclusion to which it first gives rise is that there is within me a second consciousness existing side by side with the consciousness I know.

This theory immediately evokes several criticisms. In the first place a consciousness of which its possessor knows nothing is a very different matter from the consciousness of another person. I am not directly aware of the other person's consciousness, but he is. A consciousness of which nobody is conscious seems hardly worth discussing. Certainly those who reject the idea of an unconscious system existing in the mind, will not accept in its place an "unconscious consciousness". Secondly, psycho-analysis shows that the latent mental processes which we infer are to a large extent independent of one another and ignorant of one another. So far from forming a second consciousness, they often seem so disconnected that we should be driven to postulate not only a second consciousness, but a third, a fourth, perhaps an infinite series of them—each unknown to us and to the others. This is not in itself impossible, but the idea that " my mind a kingdom is " in such a populous sense seems too far-fetched to be acceptable. Thirdly, and this is the most serious objection, we must give due weight to the fact that psycho-analysis reveals some of our latent processes as possessing peculiarities which strike us as almost incredible because they run so directly counter to all the recognized attributes of consciousness. They are not like a second consciousness at all. They seem alien to what we know of consciousness.

Rejection of the Term Subconscious

This last objection alone would justify us in rejecting the theory of a second consciousness. What we are justified in inferring is the existence within us of certain mental operations of which, while they are going on, we are not conscious. These operations are best described as " unconscious ", and the whole system of them as " the unconscious ". The terms " subconscious " and " subconsciousness " should not be used, because they are incorrect and misleading.

But is all this of any importance? Is it anything more than a rather pedantic piece of description or classification? It might be brushed aside on these grounds if we had nothing more to deal with than the well-known facts of memory and of association by means of unconscious links. But more is involved. There are other facts which compel us to distinguish between conscious and unconscious processes and which lend increased significance to the distinction. There is, notably, the peculiar fact of post-hypnotic suggestion, which has been demonstrated time and again by experiment.

Post-hypnotic Suggestion

Let us consider this experiment. The patient is put into a hypnotic state. While he is in this state, the doctor orders him to perform a certain action—not then, but at a certain definite moment after he has been awakened, say, half an hour afterwards. The patient is then roused from his hypnotic state. He is fully conscious and seems perfectly normal. He has no recollection of what took place while he was under hypnosis. Yet, at the appointed time, the impulse to perform the prescribed action comes into his mind and he performs it. He performs it consciously, but he does not know why.

There would appear to be only one way of describing what has happened : the order has been present in the patient's mind all the time, but it has been latent or unconscious until the appointed moment arrived, and then it became conscious. But when it did emerge into consciousness only part of it emerged—the idea of the action to be performed. Everything else connected with the action—the order, the influence of the doctor, the recollection of the hypnotic state—still remained unconscious.

Dynamic View

An experiment of this kind has something further to teach us. It leads us from a purely descriptive account of such phenomena to a dynamic view. For what happened at the appointed time? It was not simply that the idea of the prescribed action emerged as an object of consciousness. It emerged as a dynamic idea, an idea with active force, so that it was not merely contemplated but performed. This is the most striking point about the whole business. The doctor's order, given while the patient was under hypnosis, was the stimulus to action. Yet only the idea of the action and the urge to perform it emerged into consciousness. The order itself remained unconscious : it was at one and the same time unconscious and active.

Post-hypnotic suggestion is not, of course, a natural, spontaneous occurrence of everyday life. It is artificial, a product of the laboratory. Nevertheless, if we adopt the theory of hysterical phenomena first enunciated by Pierre Janet and afterwards elaborated by Breuer and Freud, we find ourselves in possession of a wealth of natural facts, which show clearly what is the psychological character of post-hypnotic suggestion.

Unconscious Ideas in Hysteria

The mind of the hysterical patient teams with ideas which are at once active and unconscious. All hysterical symptoms come from such ideas. The hysterical mind is ruled by them. Suppose, for instance, that a hysterical woman vomits. Her vomiting may spring from the idea of being pregnant—an idea of which she may be quite unaware, although it can easily be detected in her mind and made conscious to her by psycho-analysis. Or take another case. A hysterical patient may be subject to jerks and sudden movements, constituting what will be called " one of his fits ". In carrying them out he is not aware that they represent anything at all. He may not have any particular feeling about them. But analysis will show that, far from being arbitrary and meaningless, these movements are a sketchy reproduction of some incident in the patient's life. He has no conscious recollection of the incident while he is re-enacting it, yet there it is, operative and active during the fit.

The Strength of Unconscious Ideas

Analysis shows that in all forms of neurosis the essential fact is this preponderance of active unconscious ideas. A latent or unconscious idea is, therefore, by no means necessarily a weak one. Analysis also shows that the presence of such an idea in the mind can be established by extremely cogent, albeit indirect, evidence.

On the strength of what we have seen so far we can amplify our classification of ideas as "conscious" or "unconscious" by drawing a fundamental distinction between different kinds of unconscious or latent ideas. The theory that once prevailed was that every latent idea was so because it was weak and that as it gathered strength it became conscious. We now have reason to believe that there are some latent ideas which, however strong they have become, do not pierce their way into consciousness. Freud therefore distinguishes between two kinds of latent ideas. Those which as they grow stronger thrust themselves into consciousness, he calls *pre-conscious*. He reserves the term *unconscious* for those others which for all their intensity and activity, do not become conscious—the type which he first came to study in cases of neurosis. Thus the term *unconscious* which we have used up to now in a general descriptive sense as equivalent to "latent", becomes more precise: it comes to designate ideas which have a certain dynamic character that withholds them from consciousness despite their intensity and activity.

The Concept "Preconscious"

At this point a number of objections will probably be raised.

Instead of assuming the existence of unconscious mental elements, of which we can have no direct knowledge, would it not be better to assume that consciousness can be split up in such a way that certain ideas or other psychical elements form a consciousness apart, detached and estranged from the main body of conscious activity? There are well-known pathological cases, such as that of Dr. Azam or the cases studied by Dr. Morton

Prince, which have led serious investigators to conclude that in fact consciousness can be split up.

Rejection of the Term "Split Consciousness"

To this Freud answers: unless the word *consciousness* is to be robbed of all meaning, we must not use it to cover anything of which the owner himself is not aware. To speak of a consciousness of which the owner is not conscious is to trifle with words. Pathological cases like those cited are better described as a shifting of consciousness, rather than as a splitting of consciousness. For, after all, what happened in these cases was that the consciousness oscillated between two different psychical complexes, so that they were conscious and unconscious by turns. In any case, as was said before, those who refuse to countenance unconscious ideas are not likely to be appeased by the offering of an "unconscious consciousness".

"Gradations of Consciousness"

A second objection may be raised. Many psychologists who acknowledge the facts of psycho-analysis, try to account for them without accepting the theory of the unconscious. Desiring to find an explanation solely in terms of consciousness, they seize on the indisputable fact that there are many gradations of consciousness—gradations of intensity or clarity. Some ideas, they point out, are vivid and sharply defined in our consciousness, while others are so faint and blurred that we do not notice them. What psycho-analysts do (they argue) is to give the most dimly conscious ideas the inappropriate name of "unconscious", whereas these ideas are just as much "in consciousness" as the most vivid ones and can be rendered completely and intensely conscious if sufficient attention is paid to them.

Freud replies: the fact that there are gradations of clarity in consciousness does not prove that there are no unconscious ideas. There are many gradations of light, from dazzling glare to faintest glimmer, but we cannot therefore conclude that there is no such thing as darkness. There are varying degrees of vitality, but we cannot conclude that there is no such thing as death. Furthermore, if "what is unnoticeable" is to be included under the concept of "what is conscious", we are back at the absurdity already referred to, the absurdity of a "conscious" idea of which the possessor is not conscious. And this surely plays havoc with the one and only piece of direct and certain knowledge that we have of the mind. Finally, says Freud, the attempt to equate what psycho-analysis calls "unconscious"

"Unconscious" Not Equivalent to "Unnoticed"

with what everyday language calls "unnoticed" ignores the dynamic conditions involved in the phenomena we are seeking to illuminate—conditions which had a decisive influence on the formulation of the psycho-analytic view. For this equation of "unconscious" with "unnoticed" passes over two facts. First, if an idea of the kind which psycho-analysts have in mind is unnoticed, it will take a very considerable effort to get the attention fixed on it. Indeed, no small part of the analyst's practical work consists in trying to get the patient's attention on to the "unnoticed" idea. Secondly, when the attention has been successfully directed to it, the idea which was hitherto unnoticed is not recognized by consciousness; it often seems so alien, so utterly repugnant to everything the consciousness ever entertains, that it is instantly disavowed. This is quite a different situation from that in which the spotlight of attention moves on to an idea which has hitherto been dim and unnoticed, and renders it strong and distinct.

Freud concludes: the attempt to avoid postulating the unconscious by taking refuge in some elaboration of the fact that ideas may be hardly noticed or even entirely unnoticed is nothing more than the hugging of a preconceived belief that "mental" and "conscious" are identical terms and that their identity has been settled once and for all.

The Unconscious in Normal Psychology

A third objection is often raised. It is that psycho-analysts apply to normal psychology conclusions which are drawn chiefly from the study of pathological conditions and that therefore, while unconscious ideas may operate in the minds of neurotics or in odd circumstances like post-hypnotic suggestion, these are abnormal cases and do not justify the assumption of an unconscious at work in normal people under normal conditions. We shall meet the general objection later. For the moment it will be enough to point out that, as a matter of fact, psycho-analysts do not rest their case solely on abnormal phenomena. Psycho-analysis has shown that certain defects of function which occur every day among perfectly healthy people, e.g. slips of the tongue and errors of memory, depend on the operation of strong unconscious ideas in exactly the same way as do neurotic symptoms.

So much for objections. Let us resume our argument.

We have now refined our conception of latent processes by

differentiating between *preconscious* and *unconscious* ideas. In so doing we have passed beyond mere classification and been led to form an opinion about functional and dynamic relations in the actions of the mind. We have seen that a *preconscious* activity can pass into consciousness without difficulty, while an *unconscious* one remains so, under ordinary circumstances, and seems to be cut off from consciousness.

We do not know whether these two modes of psychical activity are in fact identical or, from the start, essentially different. Psycho-analysis does tell us, however, that it is by no means impossible for a product of unconscious mental activity to break through into consciousness, but that to do so a considerable effort is required. When we try to do it, we become aware of an obstacle; there is a distinct feeling of opposition or repugnance within ourselves, which must be overcome before we can get at it. We all know the feeling, when we are trying to recall a name, that something is holding it back. When the psycho-analyst produces this reaction in a patient, it reveals itself by unmistakable signs and he knows that he has struck against what is called the patient's *resistance* to the idea. The *unconscious* idea is kept from becoming conscious by active psychical forces which oppose its reception. These forces do not oppose the reception of *preconscious* ideas. Psycho-analysis leaves no room for doubt that this resistance to unconscious ideas is provoked by the nature and significance for us of their contents.

Resistance

Having reached this point, the most plausible theory that we can formulate is the following. (1) Unconsciousness is a normal and inevitable phase in our psychological processes. (2) Every mental act begins as an unconscious one. (3) Whether it remains so or proceeds into consciousness depends on whether it encounters resistance or not. (4) The distinction between pre-conscious and unconscious activity is not a primary one, but arises only after repulsion has sprung up. It is the fact of repulsion that gives us reason to distinguish, for the purposes of both theory and practice, between those ideas which can appear and reappear in consciousness at any moment and those which cannot.

Freud borrows an analogy—a " rough but not inadequate " one, he says—from photography. The first stage of a photograph is the " negative ". Every photograph has to pass through this stage. When they are examined, some of these negatives survive the test and are admitted to the " positive process " which results in the final picture.

Just as not every negative becomes a positive, so it is not necessary that every unconscious mental process should become a conscious one. Every mental process belongs originally to the unconscious psychical system; under certain circumstances it can pass into the conscious system.

Spatial Model of the Mind

It is convenient to describe these systems in spatial terms, although of course such a description is fictitious and crude. We may compare the unconscious system to a large ante-room, in which the various psychical elements—thoughts, emotions, impulses, and so on—jostle one another, like a crowd of suitors hoping for an audience. A doorway leads into a second and smaller apartment, a sort of audience chamber, in which the consciousness holds court. On the threshold stands a doorkeeper, who scrutinizes the would-be entrants and refuses admittance to those of whom he disapproves. Sometimes he turns a suitor back at the threshold. Sometimes, if his vigilance flags or he is slow in recognizing the suitor, he tugs one back who has already set foot inside the audience chamber. While any mental element is outside, in the unconscious, it is not visible to the consciousness, which is of course in the other room. So, to begin with, all alike are unconscious. When one of them pushes forward to the threshold and is turned back, it is denied access to the consciousness. In other words, it is rendered incapable of becoming conscious. In the terminology of psycho-analysis, it is repressed.

The Concept of Repression

When one of them has succeeded in crossing the threshold, it is capable of becoming conscious, although it has not necessarily caught the attention of consciousness. It is then what we have decided to call "preconscious". In fact, the second chamber may be suitably called the preconscious system, because whatever has entered is capable of becoming an object of consciousness, although consciousness is not aware of all the occupants of the room at any one moment. "Repressed" therefore means that the psychical element concerned is unable to pass out of the unconscious system because the doorkeeper refuses it admittance to the preconscious system. The doorkeeper is what the psycho-analyst has come to know in his attempts to treat patients as "resistance".

This little drama of fictions is admittedly crude and fantastic. It is not meant as a scientific description, but as an aid to the imagination, like Ampère's mannikin swimming in the electric current. We may improve on it later. Nevertheless, its main features—the two chambers, the doorkeeper on the threshold between them, and consciousness as a spectator at the end of the second room—do approximate in a useful degree to the facts of reality.

To have distinguished between preconscious and unconscious psychical activity and to have recognized the barrier that keeps them apart is not the final or the most important result of psycho-analytic investigations. There is one product of the mind which is familiar to most normal people and yet bears such a striking resemblance to the wildest productions of insanity that philosophers in the past found it no more intelligible than insanity itself. This product is our dreams. Now it was on the study of dreams that psycho-analysis was founded, and the interpretation of dreams is the most complete piece of work it has done up to the present.

Dreams

One of the commonest types of dream-formation is the following. During the day a train of thoughts has been set in motion in the waking mind. It has retained enough of its momentum to escape the general inhibition of interests which ushers in sleep and constitutes the mental preparation for sleep. During the night this residue of the day's mental work joins forces with one of the unconscious tendencies which have existed in the dreamer's mind since his childhood, but which are ordinarily excluded from consciousness by repression. Reinforced by this ally from the unconscious the thoughts become active again and emerge into consciousness in the shape of a dream.

Three things take place. (1) The thoughts undergo a transformation, a disguise, and a distortion. This is the work of the ally from the unconscious. (2) The thoughts occupy consciousness at a time when they ought not to do so. (3) Some part of the unconscious, which could not otherwise push its way into consciousness, succeeds in doing so.

Latent Dream Thoughts

Psycho-analysts have learnt to disentangle the residual thoughts—called the latent thoughts of the dream—and, by comparing them with the manifest dream, to estimate the changes they have undergone and the manner in which these changes have been brought about.

The latent thoughts of the dream are in no way different from the products of our ordinary conscious activity, and, in fact, they may have been conscious during some part of our waking life. They deserve the name of preconscious thoughts. But by joining forces during the night with unconscious tendencies, they have become assimilated, degraded as it were, to the level of unconscious thoughts and subject to the laws which govern unconscious activity.

Laws of Unconscious Activity

This fact enables us to discover something which we could not have learnt in any other way: that the laws of unconscious activity are very different from those of conscious activity. It enables us to ascertain some of the peculiarities of the *Unconscious*, still more of which we may hope to learn as the investigation of dream-formation progresses. The investigation is as yet in its early stages, but what we have learnt so far from the psycho-analytic study of dreams has profoundly altered our notion of the Unconscious.

Unconsciousness appeared at first as nothing more than a mysterious characteristic of individual mental acts. Such and such a piece of mental activity was unconscious instead of being conscious. Thanks to the investigation of dreams we have come to see that the fact of being unconscious places a mental act in a category which is known to us by other and more important features. Unconsciousness is not a mere isolated attribute of the single mental act, but is the sign that that act belongs to a system of mental activity which possesses quite peculiar attributes besides unconsciousness. For want of a better and less ambiguous name, we call this system "The Unconscious". The attribute of unconsciousness thus gains greatly in significance, because it is the index of much more.

"The Unconscious"

We have so far taken three main steps in developing our conception of unconsciousness. We first drew a broad distinction between those mental elements of which we are aware and those which are latent. Secondly, we distinguished between two kinds of latent elements—preconscious and unconscious proper. And now, in the third place, we have seen that unconsciousness is the badge of membership of a system of mental activity which differs significantly from the familiar conscious system.

The stress laid by psycho-analysis on the unconscious part of mental life has provoked a storm of passionate hostility. The opposition is not really due either to the difficulty of conceiving anything like the unconscious or to the relative inaccessibility of the evidence to which psycho-analysis appeals. The violence of the opposition shows that its cause is something deeper. In the course of history two other scientific theories have provoked a similar outburst of malevolence and the cause has been the same : an outrage committed by science on man's naïve self-love. The first was the discovery, associated with the name of Copernicus, that our planet is not the centre of the Universe, but only an obscure speck in a system of hardly conceivable magnitude. The second storm occurred when biological research, associated with the names of Darwin and Wallace, robbed man of his privileged position as a special creation and inflicted on him the indignity of descent from the animal world. And now comes a third blow—perhaps the bitterest of all—when psychological research alleges that the " ego " of each one of us is not even master in his own house, but must content himself with the scrappiest information about what is going on unconsciously in his own mind.

Psycho-analysts have not been the first or the only people to recommend that men should look inward and try to know themselves. But it appears to be their fate to recommend it most importunately and to support their plea with empirical evidence which affects everybody intimately. So strong are the feelings which their efforts arouse that the opponents of psycho-analysis regard themselves as absolved from the constraints alike of logic and of academic courtesy.

INSTINCTS [1]

Psychological Concepts

It is often asserted that every science should be built up on a foundation of clear and sharply-defined basic concepts. In point of fact, no science, not even the most exact, starts out from any such neat definitions. Historically, the first step in scientific activity is to describe phenomena. We then go on to group, classify, and correlate what we have described. Of course, even at the initial stage when we are describing our material, it is impossible to avoid applying to it certain abstract ideas. These ideas are certainly not derived from our experience of the material we are studying. In all probability we have taken them from a variety of sources. As a science develops, such ideas become more and more indispensable and, after much pruning and elaboration, they eventually yield its basic concepts. At first they are bound to be more or less uncertain. We are groping our way. We do not know precisely what they cover or whether they are in fact appropriate. As long as this state of affairs lasts, we keep a hand on their meaning by constantly referring to the facts we are observing. Our abstract ideas appear to be deduced from the material of observation, but in reality they often run ahead of it. We seem to divine relations between our data before we can clearly identify and establish them. Strictly speaking, these abstract ideas are in the nature of conventions. They are legitimate enough, provided our ideas are not adopted arbitrarily but are prompted by the relations we seem to find in our empirical material. As the field is more and more searchingly investigated, so we are able to formulate our concepts more and more clearly, and to modify them bit by bit till they become widely applicable and at the same time logically consistent. When at last we have done all this it may be time to crystallize them in definitions. But even then we must not take our definitions as hard and fast. The progress of science demands a permanent elasticity. Such a well-established science as physics, for example, has in our own day illustrated the way in which long-acknowledged basic concepts and definitions have to be altered to fit the advance of knowledge.

In psychology a conventional and indispensable, but still

[1] Coll. Pap., vol. iv, pp. 60–67 [Instincts and their vicissitudes].
Int. J. Psa., xxi, part i, pp. 31 ff. [An outline of Psycho-Analysis].

rather obscure, basic concept is that of *instinct.* Let us try to see what this concept covers by approaching it from different angles.

Instinct and Reflex

Let us start from the point of view of physiology. Physiology has acquainted us with the concept of stimuli and the scheme of the reflex arc, according to which a stimulus impinging on living tissue or nervous substance *from the outside world* is discharged by action *towards the outside world.* The action serves the purpose of withdrawing the substance affected from the range of operation of the stimulus. Blinking or dropping a hot plate are examples.

Stimuli

Now what is the relation between "instinct" and "stimulus"? We might be inclined to say that an instinct is one particular kind of stimulus—a stimulus to the mind. But, on second thoughts, can we identify "stimulus to the mind" and "instinct"? Obviously not, because while some stimuli to the mind are of what we should unhesitatingly call instinctual origin others operate far more like physiological stimuli. A strong light striking upon the eye may be a stimulus to the mind, but it is not a stimulus of instinctual origin. On the other hand, when the mucous membrane of the œsophagus becomes parched or when a gnawing makes itself felt in the stomach (assuming that these internal processes form the organic basis of thirst and hunger) the stimulus is of instinctual origin.

Among stimuli which operate on our minds we have then to distinguish between those which are of instinctual origin and others which are physiological. We see, first, that a stimulus of instinctual origin arises, not in the outside world, but from within the organism itself. Its mental effect and the actions necessary to discharge it differ accordingly. In the second place, everything essential about response to an external stimulus is covered by the assumption that it functions as a single appropriate action. For example, you grasp a hot plate and then drop it. External impacts may, of course, be repeated and their force may be cumulative, but that makes no difference to our conception of the process or to the actions necessary for getting rid of the stimulus. With an

Constant Action of Instincts

instinct the situation is different. An instinct never acts as an isolated momentary impact, like the burn of the hot plate, but always as a constant force. Since it operates from within the organism there can be no question of withdrawing out of its range. You can detach yourself from the hot plate; you cannot detach yourself from your hunger or thirst. An instinct has to be satisfied somehow or other. It is in the nature of a need. In fact " need " is a better term for a stimulus of instinctual origin. And it can only be satisfied by bringing about a suitable and adequate change in the inner source of stimulation.

Need and Satisfaction

Let us picture the situation of an almost completely helpless organism, as yet unorientated in the world. Stimuli impinge on its nervous tissue. It soon begins to make a first discrimination and a first orientation. It discovers that certain stimuli can be avoided by an action of the muscles—withdrawal or flight. At the same time it discovers other stimuli against which no such action is of any avail, whose urgency is unaffected by muscular attempts to get away. It attributes the first sort of stimuli to an outside world. Stimuli of the second sort are the signs of an inner world, the evidences of instinctual needs. In the efficacy or inefficacy of its muscular activity the organism discovers a criterion for distinguishing between outer and inner.

Distinction between Outer and Inner World

Our first conception of the essence of an instinct thus arises from a consideration of its two main characteristics—that it originates in sources of stimulation within the organism, and that it appears, not as a sudden and transitory impact, but as a constant force. From these we deduce a third characteristic, that no action of withdrawal or flight avails against it.

In this brief preliminary inquiry we have already accepted as basic concepts certain conventions and we have applied them to the material we have obtained empirically. Furthermore, we have made use of various complicated postulates to guide us in dealing with psychological phenomena. The most important of these postulates is of a biological nature. It involves the concept of purpose, of the adaptation of means to an end. It runs as follows: the nervous system is an apparatus whose function is to annul or neutralize stimuli which impinge upon it, or at least to reduce excitation to the minimum possible. It is an apparatus which would, if such a thing were feasible, maintain itself in a completely unstimulated condition. Its ideal, so to speak, is a world without stimuli. The idea so formulated is pretty indefinite, but let that pass for the moment. Let us assume that the task of the nervous system is, broadly speaking, to master stimuli. It is

Task of the Nervous System

at once obvious that the simple physiological reflex scheme becomes vastly complicated once we introduce instincts. Stimuli from outside impose one single task on the organism—to get out of their way. At the impact of the stimulus muscular movements are carried out. One of them succeeds because it is the most appropriate. It is transmitted as a hereditary disposition. But instinctual stimuli, originating as they do within the organism itself, cannot be dealt with by this mechanism. The demands they make on the nervous system are therefore much greater. They force it to carry out complicated chains of activity so as to make such changes in the outer world as will enable it to satisfy the inner source of stimulation. Most important of all, these instinctual stimuli, because they keep up an incessant and inescapable barrage of stimulation, compel the nervous system to abandon its aim of annulling stimuli and instead to come to terms with them. We are probably justified in concluding that instincts, and not external stimuli, have been the driving force behind the development of the nervous system to its remarkable level of efficiency. This conclusion would not, of course, rule out the possibility that the instincts themselves are, at least in part, the precipitates of various forms of external stimulation, which in the course of evolution have brought about modifications in the organism.

There is another postulate which can hardly be avoided. It is the so-called pleasure principle. Even the most highly developed mental apparatus is automatically regulated by feelings of pleasure and pain. We therefore postulate that these feelings reflect success or failure in mastering stimuli. This is certainly true in the sense that unpleasant or painful feelings are associated with an increase in stimulation, and pleasurable feelings with a decrease. Once again the formulation is vague. We shall have to leave it so until we are in a position to say what sort of relation exists between pleasure and pain on the one hand and, on the other, fluctuations in the strength of stimuli which affect mental life. Of one thing we may be sure: many kinds of relation are possible, some of them anything but simple.

Pleasure and Pain

Instinct a Borderland Concept

So much for instinct from the physiological point of view. If we now consider mental life from a biological point of view we may say that an instinct appears to be a borderland concept between the mental and the physical. It is the mental representative of stimuli which originate within the organism and penetrate to the mind ; at the same time it is a measure of the demand made upon the energy of the mind by virtue of its connection with the body.

In the light of what we have seen so far we can discuss a number of terms which are used with reference to the concept of an instinct.

Impetus of an Instinct

First its impetus. By this we mean its driving element—the amount of force which it represents or the measure of the demand it makes on energy. To impel or urge or drive is the very essence of an instinct. If we speak of " passive " instincts we are speaking inaccurately. We can only mean instincts whose aim is passive. The instinct itself cannot be other than active.

Aim of an Instinct

The aim of every instinct is to obtain satisfaction. This can only be done by ending the state of stimulation in the source of the instinct. But, while this is always the final aim of an instinct, there may be a variety of ways of achieving it. In other words, an instinct may have various intermediate aims which are less remote than the final aim. And these may be capable of combination or interchange. We know, too, from experience that instincts may be inhibited in respect of their aim : some degree of progress towards satisfaction takes place and then inhibition or deflection intervenes. Even in such cases, however, partial satisfaction is presumably achieved.

Object of an Instinct

The object of an instinct is defined by Freud as " that in or through which it can achieve its aim ". Nothing about an instinct is so variable as its object. The object is not connected with it from the start, but becomes attached to it because it proves capable of giving satisfaction. The object need not be anything external to the organism. It may be part of the organism itself. Nor need it always be the same. In the course of the vicissitudes which the instinct undergoes during a lifetime, it may repeatedly change the object to which it attaches itself. Indeed this capacity for displacement is an extremely important factor in the whole story of instincts. Again a single object may serve to satisfy several instincts at one and the same time—a phenomenon which Adler terms a " confluence " of instincts. If an instinct forms an exceptionally close attachment to a particular object, as occurs quite often in the very early stages of its development, we speak of a " fixation ". Once a fixation takes place it sets up a powerful resistance against any detachment from the particular object and so puts an end to the instinct's mobility.

Source of an Instinct

Another term used is the *source* of an instinct. By this we mean the process in some organ or part of the body from which arises a stimulus that is represented in mental life as an instinct. It is not known whether this process is always of a chemical nature or whether it may also correspond to the release of other forces, e.g. mechanical forces. This is a matter which lies outside the scope of psychology. It is true that the source of an instinct within the body gives it its distinct and essential character and may often be inferred from its aims. But what concerns the psychologist is its manifestation in mental life, where we only know it by its aims.

Quality of Instincts

Is there any reason to think that the different instincts operate on the mind in qualitatively different ways? Freud thinks there is not and that it is sufficient to assume that the instincts are qualitatively alike. The effect they produce would then be due to the quantity of excitation accompanying them and perhaps also to certain functions of this quantity. The difference in the mental effects they produce may be traced to the difference in their sources. In any case we shall only see the significance of the problem of quality in a later connection.

Number of Instincts

A favourite topic of discussion has been the number of instincts that we ought to postulate. Different authors have drawn up lists of varying lengths. Sometimes the same author, e.g. McDougall, has given different lists at different times. Obviously the subject lends itself to endless arbitrary list-making. On the other hand the concept is a valid one, and it is perfectly legitimate for anyone to speak of particular instincts, such as an instinct of play or destruction or a social instinct, when the subject demands it and the limitations of psychological analysis permit it. What has led to the drawing up of such detailed lists of instincts is the fact that instinctual motivations are highly specialized. The question arises, however, whether the number cannot be reduced by an analysis in terms of their sources, so that the name could be restricted to those primal instincts which cannot be resolved into anything else.

Instinct Theory

Freud gave a great deal of thought to this problem. After what he describes as " long doubts and vacillations " he came to the conclusion that it was not necessary to assume the existence of more than two fundamental instincts. These he called (1) Eros or the love instinct, and (2) the destructive or death instinct.

The aim of the first is to bind together—to establish and maintain ever greater unities. The instincts of self-preservation and the preservation of the species, although in a sense they clash, fall within the bounds of Eros. So do ego-love and object-love.

The aim of the second fundamental instinct is to undo connections and so to destroy. Its final aim may be presumed to be the reduction of living things to an inorganic state.

In biological functions these two fundamental instincts sometimes work against one another, sometimes combine with one another. The act of eating, for instance, consists in destroying an object for the purpose of incorporating it; the sexual act consists in an aggression whose purpose is the most intimate union. From this interplay of the two fundamental instincts with and against one another arises the whole endless variety of human life.

THE SEXUAL INSTINCT

Definition

The popular view of human sexual life is that it consists essentially in each person's impulse to bring his own genitals into contact with those of a person of the opposite sex. With this are associated, as foreplay and accessory phenomena, such acts as kissing the other's body, inspecting and touching it. It is commonly thought, moreover, that this impulse makes its appearance at puberty, when the individual attains sexual maturity, and that it serves the purposes of reproduction.

Certain facts, however, which do not fit into the framework of this narrow view have always been known. In the first place there is the striking fact that people exist who are only attracted by the persons and genitals of members of their own sex. A second and no less remarkable fact is that there are people—known as " perverts "—whose desires are in all respects like sexual desires, except that they disregard the sexual organs and their normal use. And thirdly, there is the fact that many children (who on that account are looked on as degenerates) take a very early interest in their genitals and show signs of excitation in them.

Findings of Psycho-analysis

It was partly on account of these three neglected facts that psycho-analysis joined issue with the popular view of sexuality. When it contradicted that view it aroused astonishment and incredulity and was hotly denied. The main findings of psycho-analysis on this subject may be summarized in three points.

(*a*) Sexual life does not start at puberty. Its first manifestations may be clearly seen shortly after birth.

(*b*) It is a mistake to restrict the idea of sexuality to activities connected with the genitals. Sexuality is a wider concept and embraces many activities which have no connection with the genitals.

(*c*) The fundamental function of sexuality is to obtain pleasure from zones of the body. This function is later brought into the service of reproduction, but the two functions often fail to coincide completely.

Infantile Sexuality

The first of these three assertions is the one which has caused the greatest surprise and interest. Because the popular view limited sexuality to genital activity and associated it primarily with reproduction, the suggestion that a baby could have any sexual life seemed both preposterous and repulsive. Yet it has been found that infants display bodily activity which we should not hesitate to call sexual if we could forget the popular idea of sex, and which is connected with mental phenomena that occur later on in adult love, such as fixation on a particular object, jealousy, and so on. Observation of infants shows, too, that these phenomena form part of a regular process of development. They emerge in early childhood, increase steadily, and reach a climax towards the end of the fifth year. Then a lull sets in, during which much is unlearnt and undone. This lull, this period of latency, lasts till puberty, when sexual life again bursts into flower.

Latency Period

In human beings the onset of sexual life thus occurs in two stages, separated by a considerable gap of time. There is no such thing in any other species, and it evidently has an important bearing on the origin of man as a creature so remarkably different from other creatures. Man is descended from mammals which reach sexual maturity once and for all at the age of five. It has been suggested that some great external influence intervened in the case of man to hold up this straightforward development of sexuality. This interruption may also be connected with some other transformations which distinguish the sexual life of man from that of the animals. There is, for instance, the fact that man is not seasonal in his desire and capacity for sexual intercourse.

Whatever its full significance may be, the fact remains that in man alone sexual life has a double onset. Connected with this is another fact on whose importance psycho-analysis lays great stress. With very few exceptions the events of the early period of sexuality are forgotten. Infantile amnesia removes them from the reach of consciousness.

These views are the basis of the psycho-analytical account of the origin of neuroses and it is from them that the technique of analytical therapy is derived. In the course tracing the process of development in the first few years of life psycho-analysis has also come upon evidence for yet other conclusions.

Erotogenic Zones

In Freud's view, as we have seen, the basic function of sexuality is to obtain pleasure from zones of the body. He calls any zone which is capable of giving pleasure " erotogenic ". Now the first organ to manifest itself as an erotogenic zone is the mouth. From birth onwards it furnishes pleasure and makes libidinal demands on the mind. The baby's mental activity is concentrated, to begin with, on the absorbing business of satisfying the needs of that zone. These needs, of course, serve the purpose of self-preservation. The baby sucks in the first place to get nourishment. But physiology must not be confused with psychology. Although

Oral Phase

the sucking originates from and is stimulated by the taking of nourishment, the baby's persistance in sucking shows signs at an early stage of an enjoyment which is independent of nourishment. It is seeking to obtain another form of pleasure besides. And for that reason what the baby is doing is described by Freud as sexual within his wider conception of the term.

Sadistic-Anal Phase

The first phase of sexual life is thus the oral phase. But already during the oral phase there are sporadic signs of other impulses. These are sadistic impulses and they begin to occur with the appearance of the teeth. Their manifestations increase during the second phase, which Freud calls the sadistic-anal phase because in it the infant seeks satisfaction in aggression and in the excretory function. Freud includes these aggressive impulses among the manifestations of the libido on the hypothesis that sadism is an instinctual fusion of purely libidinal and purely destructive impulses—a fusion which, once established, persists without interruption.[1]

Phallic Phase

In the third phase the infant's interest is attracted by the zone which plays the central part in adult sexual life. This phase foreshadows the final shape of sexual life and bears a considerable resemblance to it. But, according to Freud, there is this striking difference : what arouses interest is not the genitals of both sexes, but only those of the male, and in particular the phallus. Hence he calls this the phallic phase. The female genitals remain for a long time unknown. The child, in his efforts to understand sexual processes, very often hits upon the venerable cloacal theory—a theory which has a genetic justification. He does not hit upon the correct theory. Moreover, the alleged signs of vaginal excitation in female infants are

[1] In this connection the problem arises whether the satisfaction of purely destructive impulses can be felt as pleasure, whether such a thing as pure destruction without any libidinal component ever occurs. Freud's conclusion is that satisfaction of what remains in the ego of the death instinct seems not to produce feelings of pleasure. He takes masochism to be a fusion exactly analogous to sadism.

probably signs of excitation of the clitoris ; and, since the clitoris is the female organ corresponding to the penis, we may continue to speak of the third phase as phallic.

In the phallic phase the sexuality of early childhood attains its peak and draws to its decline. From that point onwards the development of boys and girls follows different paths. Both started by thinking a great deal about sex and by assuming the universal presence of the penis. Now they proceed in different directions because the one sex possesses and the other does not possess this organ. The boy enters the Oedipus phase. He begins to touch and handle his penis. Phantasies arise in his mind in which he carries out some kind of activity with it in relation to his mother. Finally, says Freud, " owing to the combined effect of a threat of castration and the spectacle of women's lack of a penis, he experiences the greatest trauma of his life and this introduces the period of latency with all its consequences."

Oedipus Phase

With the girl what happens is this : she would like to do the same as the boy, but she is forced to realize her lack of a penis, or rather the inferiority of her clitoris. This realization has a permanent effect on the development of her character. Often, after this first disappointment in rivalry, she turns away from sexual life altogether.

The three phases which Freud has picked out and named are not to be understood as following one another with neat mechanical precision. One of them may appear side by side with another.

The separate component instincts at the outset pursue their pleasure independently. It is not till the phallic phase that there are any signs of the subordination of other trends to the primacy of the genitals. In that phase the diffused impulse towards pleasure begins to be co-ordinated into the specifically sexual function. This process of organization reaches completion with puberty, in the genital phase. When this fourth phase is established what happens to the tendencies which were involved in the earlier phases? Many of them persist in their own right. Others of them are enrolled in the total sexual function as preparatory or auxiliary acts, whose satisfaction produces what is known as " fore-pleasure ". Other tendencies, again, are rejected and find no place in the sexual function as it comes to be established. They may be suppressed or repressed ; or they may be diverted to

Genital Phase

other uses, forming traits of character or undergoing sublimation with a displacement of their aims.

Disturbances of Sexual Development

The process of organization which constitutes the fourth phase of libidinal development is not always carried through without a hitch. Inhibitions often occur and then exhibit themselves as disturbances of the normal sexual development. The libido may fail to detach itself from one of its earlier objects and through this fixation a trend persists independently of the normal sexual aims. This is known as *perversion*. Manifest homosexuality is an example. Analysis shows that in every case there existed at one time a homosexual attachment to some object, an attachment which in most cases persists in a latent state. The conditions for bringing about a normal development are seldom completely present or completely absent. The final outcome depends in each case on a balance of conditions. The organization of the genital phase is therefore apt to be impared by the lagging behind of portions of the libido which remain fixated to objects and aims that belong to earlier phases. The result is that if genital satisfaction is not obtained or if there are difficulties in the world in which the individual lives, there is a tendency for the libido to revert to earlier forms of satisfaction. This is called *regression*.

Regression

The study of the sexual functions gives us the first intimation of two pieces of knowledge which further study shows to have significance over the whole field of psychology. First, the phenomena that we observe, both normal and abnormal, call for description from two points of view. Freud describes these as the point of view of dynamics and the point of view of economics, e.g. in the case we have been discussing, the quantitative distribution of the libido. Secondly, the origins of the disturbances we are studying are to be sought in the history of the individual's development in the early years of his life.

Object Relationships

To a child the earliest erotic object is the mother's breast that feeds him. On the soil of a satisfied need for food, love grows. At the outset the child does not distinguish his mother's breast from his own body. What causes him to make a distinction is the fact that he misses the breast so often. When he realizes that it is not part of him, but outside, the breast becomes an " object " which carries with it part of his attachment. Later on this first object expands into

Mother and Child

the whole person of the mother, who not only feeds him, but looks after him in every way. She is the source of numerous other physical sensations, some of them pleasant and some unpleasant. In this dual relationship lies the root of the mother's unique importance. " By her care of the child's body," says Freud, " she becomes his first seducer." The child's relation to his or her mother, as the first and strongest object of love, becomes the prototype of all subsequent love relationships. The character of all later relationships is established by that first unparalleled love relationship. The phylogenetic foundation outweighs all the chance variations and incidents of individual experience. Whether the child is breast-fed or bottle-fed, whether he or she receives all the tenderness of a mother's care or not, the development is the same. If anything, it is the child who has been deprived of breast and care who will later on have the greater longing. And no matter how long a child is fed at his mother's breast, he will always feel that his feeding was cut short too soon.

Oedipus Complex

These considerations of the relationship between mother and child prepare us for the intensity of what Freud has called the Oedipus complex. Here is his account of it:

" When a boy, from about two or three years old, enters upon the phallic phase of his libidinal development, feels pleasurable sensations in his sexual organ and learns to procure these at will by manual stimulation, he becomes his mother's lover. He desires to possess her physically in the ways which he has derived from his observations and intuitive surmises of sexual life; he tries to seduce her by showing her the male organ of which he is the proud owner. In a word, his early awakened masculinity makes him seek to assume, in relation to her, the place belonging to his father, who has hitherto been an envied model on account of the physical strength which he displays and of the authority in which he is clothed. His father now becomes a rival who stands in his way and whom he would like to push aside. If when his father is absent he is able to share his mother's bed and if when his father returns he is once more banished from it, his gratification when his father vanishes and his disappointment when he reappears are deeply felt experiences."

This tale of desire and rivalry is the content of the Oedipus complex. The name is taken, of course, from the Greek legend, in which Freud saw childhood experience reproduced in the guise of adult dramatic action.

It was Freud's opinion that, under the conditions of our civilization, the Oedipus complex frequently works itself out disastrously. The mother finds herself faced with a problem, and her solution of the problem has a lasting influence on the boy's development. She understands that the boy's sexual excitement refers to her and she decides that this state of affairs is wrong and must be stopped. So she forbids the boy to handle his genitals. Her prohibition does not stop him, but at most leads to some modification in his method of procuring pleasurable sensations. Eventually she adopts the sternest measure she can think of: she threatens to take away from him the organ with which he is defying her. To make her threat as plausible and frightening as possible she says that she will tell his father and that he will cut the penis off. Even so the threat, by itself, is not completely convincing: the boy does not really think that it could happen. But there is one thing that can make the threat convincing and that is the sight of female genitals. If the boy happens to see female genitals, or has already seen them, he realizes that it is possible to be without the supremely valued organ. He takes what he has been told seriously and supposes that he has seen a case where the threat has actually been carried out. The fear engendered sets up the castration complex and this shock is the severest trauma of a boy's childhood.

Castration Complex

The castration theme has its place, too, in the Oedipus legend according to Freud. For after Oedipus had discovered his crime he punished himself with blindness, and blindness, on the evidence of analysis, is a symbolical substitute in dreams for castration.

The extraordinarily terrifying effect of the threat of castration may be due in part to a phylogenetic memory trace from the pre-history of the human family. This is a possibility that Freud is not prepared to rule out. If true it would be a trace left in the memory from a time when the jealous father would actually castrate his son so as to preserve his own monopoly of a woman or women. Freud thought that the ancient custom of circumcision was a symbolic substitute for castration and, like the puberty rights of many primitive peoples, expressed the son's subjection to the will of his father.

As has been said above Freud considered the effects of the

Oedipus complex in our civilization to be disastrous. He pointed out, however, that no investigation had been made of the course which the events we have been considering take in the case of peoples and civilizations which do not frown upon masturbation among children. In our civilization the far-reaching and incalculable effects of the castration threat include a decisive influence on a boy's relations not only with his father and mother, but later on with men and women in general. Under stress of the first shock to his masculinity he gives up possession of his mother more or less completely rather than risk the loss of his sexual organ. His whole subsequent sexual life often lies permanently under the weight of the prohibition. If there is a strong feminine component in his character it is strengthened. He adopts towards his father the kind of passive attitude which he ascribes to his mother. The threat to his masculinity causes him to give up masturbation, but he does not give up the imaginations that accompany it. Indeed, since they alone remain to him he seeks gratification in them more than ever. He continues in these fantasies to identify himself with his father, but at the same time, and perhaps more and more predominantly, he also identifies himself with his mother. The products and derivatives of these early masturbatory fantasies make their way as a rule into his later ego, modified in various ways, and play their part in the formation of his character. On the one hand the feminine streak in him is encouraged. On the other fear and hatred of his father increase. His baffled masculinity takes refuge in a defiant attitude towards his father, and this in turn dictates his later behaviour in human society. His early erotic fixation on his mother often leaves its mark as an excessive dependence upon her, which afterwards takes the form of a general submissiveness towards women. He no longer ventures to love his mother. Yet he cannot risk not being loved by her for fear that she might betray him to his father and to the menace of castration. The whole experience, which, with all its antecedents and consequences is much more elaborate than the account that has just been given, is eventually repressed with a great deal of energy. But the conflicting impulses and reactions continue their existence in the unconscious, biding their time to disturb the later development of the ego. Their opportunity comes after puberty. The bodily process of sexual maturity then infuses new life into the old libidinal fixations which, to all appearances, had been surmounted, and sexual

Character Formation

life is revealed as inhibited, incoherent, and torn by mutually conflicting impulses.

The threat of castration, it is true, does not always have such a terrible effect on a boy's budding sexual life. How much damage is done and how much avoided will depend, once again, on a balance of conditions. The whole experience is certainly the most fateful experience and the greatest problem of early life. It is also the main source of inadequacy later on. But it is so completely forgotten by the individual himself that its reconstruction in the course of psycho-analysis always meets with the patient's most stubborn incredulity. The resistance which the adult shows to this subject is so great that every effort is made to silence any mention of it. The most obvious reminders of it are met with a quite extraordinary intellectual blindness. For

The Oedipus Legend

example, it is frequently denied that the legend of King Oedipus has any connection with the construction made by psycho-analysis. The story, it is alleged, was entirely different, because Oedipus did not know that it was his father whom he killed and his mother whom he married. To brush the story aside in this way is to overlook the fact that a poetic handling of the material requires a distortion of this kind. It also overlooks the fact that the poetic handling adds no subject matter foreign to the theme, but confines itself to a skilful manipulation of the inherent factors. The ignorance of Oedipus is an entirely valid and appropriate method of representing dramatically the unconsciousness into which, for adults, the whole experience has fallen. The doom of the oracle, which strictly speaking should clear the hero of guilt, is a dramatic recognition of the inevitability of the fate which has condemned every son to experience the Oedipus complex.

Hamlet

The champions of psycho-analysis have not been slow to point out that there is another famous hero of drama whose enigma can be solved by a reference to the Oedipus complex. Hamlet came to grief over the task of punishing someone else for doing what his own Oedipus wishes had pointed to. The literary world showed little understanding of the suggestion when it was put forward and a strong resolution to keep its infantile repressions intact.

Freud points out that over a century before the birth of psycho-analysis the French philosopher Diderot had an insight into the Oedipus complex when he expressed the difference between the primitive world and the civilized world in the following sentence: "If the little savage were left to himself, keeping all his foolishness and adding to the small sense of a suckling the violent passions of a man of thirty, he would strangle his father and lie with his mother."

Envy of Penis

So much for the effects on a boy. The effects of the castration complex on a little girl are more uniform and no less profound. Her situation is, of course, different because she has no need to fear the amputation of a penis. What she has to react to is the fact of never having been given one. From the start she envies boys its possession. Her whole development may be said to be influenced by this envy. She begins by making unsuccessful attempts to do the same as boys. Later she attempts, with more success, to compensate herself for her deficiency and these efforts may lead ultimately to a normal feminine attitude. If during the phallic phase she tries to gratify herself like a boy by the manual stimulation of her genitals, she is unlikely to procure sufficient satisfaction and her impression of inferiority may extend to her whole self. As a rule she soon gives up seeking physical pleasure in this way, which is not only unrewarding in itself but reminds her of the superiority of her brother or other little boys, and she turns away for the time being from sexuality altogether.

If a little girl sticks to her original desire to become a boy she will in extreme cases end by becoming a manifest homosexual. Or if she does not go as far as that, she will imitate masculine traits in later life—in manner, dress, choice of occupation, and so on. That is one road of development. The other road is this. Envious of the penis, the girl sees her mother as responsible for sending her into the world so inadequately equipped. In her resentment she turns away from her and makes someone else—her father—the main object of her love. But if one has lost a love-object, the most obvious reaction is to identify oneself with it—to replace it from within so to speak. This natural mechanism now comes to the little girl's aid. Instead of making her mother the principal object of her love she identifies herself with her mother. She has always made a little mother of herself in her play. She now tries to put herself in her mother's place in real earnest in relation to her father. The result is that she begins to entertain a hatred of her mother, not only from mortification over the inadequate equipment for which she blames her, but from jealousy as well. The first content of her desire in this new relation to her father may be a wish to have his penis at her command ; it culminates, however, in another wish—to have a baby from him as a present.

The relation between the Oedipus complex and the castration complex is exactly reversed in the case of women and of men. In men the threat of castration brings the Oedipus complex to an end. In women the lack of a penis is what drives them into their Oedipus complex. It does little harm to a woman if she continues in her feminine Oedipus attitude. (The name of " Electra complex " has been suggested for the feminine version.) If she continues in this attitude she will choose a husband for his fatherly characteristics and will be ready to submit to his authority. Her original and insatiable desire to possess a penis may be satisfied if she succeeds in expanding her love for the organ to the entire man who bears it, in the same way as earlier she extended her love from the breast to her mother.

Any practising psycho-analyst will testify that the mental formations which he has found hardest to influence in his patients and indeed altogether least accessible are the same : in a woman the desire for a penis ; in a man the feminine attitude towards his own sex whose precondition we have seen to be the shock to his masculinity.

" CIVILIZED " SEXUAL MORALITY AND MODERN NERVOUSNESS [1]

In Freud's opinion our civilization is, generally speaking, founded on the suppression of instincts. The achievements of our civilization, both material and ideal, are derived from the fact that each individual contributes some renunciation of his aggressive, domineering, and vindictive tendencies. What has induced individuals to make this renunciation? Over and above the struggle for existence, in which group solidarity is an advantage, the chief motive has been family feeling, a feeling whose roots go back to the earliest love experiences. This renunciation has been a progressive one in the evolution of civilization. The single steps which marked its progress were sanctioned by religion. Each item of instinctual satisfaction which the individual denied himself was offered to the Divinity as a sacrifice. The benefit which thus accrued to the community was pronounced " Holy ". The individual who cannot bend his nature to comply with the required suppressions becomes a criminal, an outlaw, unless his position in the community or his outstanding talents enable him to hold his own—in which case he becomes a hero or great man.

The sexual instinct, with its many component impulses, is probably more strongly developed in man than in most of the higher animals. In any case it is more constant since it has almost entirely lost the seasonal character which it has in animals. It also shows a marked ability in man to change its aim without substantially losing in intensity, and so it places an extraordinary amount of energy at the disposal of " cultural " activities. This capacity for turning from its original aim to some other aim which is not sexual, though it is psychically related, is called the capacity for sublimation. It is of the utmost value for civilization. It is the favourable aspect of that flexibility which distinguishes man from the animals with their rigid pattern of development. The unfavourable aspect is the stubborn tendency of the sexual instinct to get fixated, which not only prevents it from being used as a source of energy for other activities, but occasionally leads to degeneration in so-called abnormalities.

Sublimation

[1] Coll. Pap., vol. ii, pp. 82–99 [" Civilized " sexual morality and modern nervousness].

It seems probable that the original strength of the sexual instinct varies from individual to individual. It is certain that the capacity for sublimation varies. It seems as though an individual's original constitution sets a limit to the amount of sexual impulse that can be sublimated and turned to other uses. Over and above this the forces of environment and of intellectual influence, e.g. in the course of education, play their part in deciding how much is in fact sublimated. Unlimited sublimation is undoubtedly impossible, as impossible as it is to transmute heat illimitably into mechanical power. Some degree of direct sexual satisfaction appears to be absolutely necessary for by far the majority of human beings. The individual need may vary, but its frustration will revenge itself. It will produce manifestations which will be properly regarded as illness, both because they hamper and impair functional activity and because they are painful to the individual himself.

Auto-erotism

We should bear in mind the fact which we have already considered that the sexual instinct in man aims originally at procuring particular kinds of pleasure, not at procreation. We saw that in infancy it obtained gratification, not only in connection with the genitals, but also from other zones of the body. In infancy it is able to disregard any other than these easily accessible objects. This is called the stage of auto-erotism. It is part of the first steps in a child's upbringing to narrow it down, because if it were to continue it would render the sexual instinct uncontrollable and unserviceable in later life. From auto-erotism the sexual instinct passes on to object-love, from the autonomy of the erotogenic zones to the subordination of these to the primacy of the genitals, which serve the purpose of procreation. As this development proceeds part of the self-obtained sexual excitation is checked as being of no use for the function of procreation. Under favourable circumstances this surplus energy is diverted by way of sublimation to other uses. The energies released for "cultural" development are thus to a large extent made available through the suppression of the so-called perverse forms of sexual excitation.

Stages in Sexual Morality

We may distinguish three stages in cultural development corresponding with the development of the sexual instinct as we have traced it. The first stage would be that in which no ban is laid on the free exercise of the sexual impulses in regard to aims which do not lead to procreation. The second stage would be characterized by the suppression of all forms of sexual impulse except the form which serves the purpose of procreation. In the third stage we should find yet a further limitation: the only sexual aim which is permitted is *legitimate* procreation. This third stage represents the current sexual morality of our own civilization.

Admittedly the restrictions of this third stage prove too much for many people. But even the second stage makes demands to which a number of people are unequal. There are whole classes of persons in whom the development from auto-erotism to object-love has not been properly completed. This failure to pass on to object-love, whose aim is genital union with a person of the opposite sex, gives rise to two kinds of harmful deviation from "civilized" sexuality. These two forms of deviation are related to one another almost as positive to negative. (They are not, it should be noted, the only forms of disorder; we are disregarding here those persons with an uncontrollable sexual instinct, for instance.) First, there are the different varieties of perverts; their trouble is that an infantile fixation on one of the preliminary sexual aims has blocked the way to the establishment of the primacy of the reproductive function. Secondly, there are the inverts or homosexuals; their trouble is that, in some way as yet not fully understood, the sexual aim has been deflected from the opposite sex to their own. The harmful results of these two forms of disturbance are less than might have been expected, thanks to the fact that the sexual instinct is not a simple or single-track thing, but a complicated co-ordination of component parts. This makes it possible for the sexual life eventually to find expression in some form or other, even if one or more of the components has failed to develop normally. As a matter of fact, in the case of homosexuals there is often a strong tendency to cultural sublimation.

Perverts and Inverts

Perversion and inversion, if strongly developed and especially if they have become exclusive, tend to make their victims socially unadaptable and unhappy. Those who differ constitutionally from their fellows in this respect tend to suffer in proportion to the strength or weakness of their sexual impulse in an absolute sense. If the impulse is comparatively weak perverts generally succeed in suppressing those tendencies which conflict with the moral requirements of the surrounding civilization. And this is the sum total of their achievement, because they expend in doing so all the energies which they might otherwise have turned to cultural activity. They are, in Freud's phrase, "at once inwardly stunted and outwardly crippled." When the sexual instinct is very strong but perverted there are two possible results. In the first case the afflicted person remains perverted and has to bear the consequences of his departure from the prevailing level of culture. The second is much more interesting. Here the perverse impulse is suppressed under pressure of education and the demands of society, but the suppression is not a true one.

Neuroses

Freud describes it as "a miscarriage of suppression". The inhibited impulses do not find expression in their direct and obvious form—to that extent the inhibition is successful. But they do find expression in other and indirect ways which do quite as much harm to the person concerned and render him quite as useless to society as expression in the original form would have done. This failure is in the long run far more unfortunate than the success in repression is fortunate. In place of the direct expression of the forbidden impulses, substitute manifestations appear and these constitute what are called neuroses, in particular psycho-neuroses. Neurotics are defined by Freud as "that class of people, naturally rebellious, with whom the pressure of cultural demands succeeds only in an apparent suppression of their instincts". The suppression, moreover, becomes less and less effective as time goes on. To co-operate in the life of a civilized community, therefore, means for them a great expenditure of energy combined with inner impoverishment. At times they cannot keep it up: these are their periods of illness. The neuroses stand to the perversions as negative to positive because in them the repressed perverse tendencies find their way into expression from the unconscious, and because they contain the same tendencies in a state of repression that manifest perverts exhibit.

Everyone finds that at some time or other he would like to kick over the traces and defy the demands of civilization. For most people there is a limit beyond which their constitution cannot comply with these demands. What happens to those who strain after a higher standard than their constitution allows is that they become neurotics. For them the better is indeed the enemy of the good. Had they remained less perfect it would have been happier for them. The positive-negative relation between pervertion and neurosis is often exemplified in the case of members of one and the same family. It has frequently been observed that where a brother is sexually perverted the sister (who as a woman is endowed with a weaker sexual instinct) becomes a neurotic, with symptoms that express the same tendencies as the perversion of her brother. Accordingly in many families the men are healthy but immoral, while the women are high-principled and over-refined but neurotic. It is one of the injustices of social life that the standard of sexual behaviour which civilization demands should bear heavily on one person and not on another: one can attain it without effort, while another finds it a severe strain on his resources of mind and character. Of course, in practice, the injustice is often evened out by disregard of morality.

So far we have been speaking of the second stage of cultural development, which we postulated as prohibiting "perverse" sexual activity but permitting freedom of "normal" sexual intercourse. And we have seen that even this degree of restriction rules out a number of people as perverse and drives a certain number of others, who try against their constitutions not to be perverse, into neurosis. If we now turn to the third stage of cultural development, which we postulated as imposing yet a further restriction on sexual freedom, we shall not be surprised at what we find. The standard demanded at this stage rules out all sexual activity which does not take place within authorized marriage. The number of natures whose strong sexual instinct leads them to rebel against this restriction is very much greater. And the number of weaker natures who take refuge in neurosis as a way out of the conflict between society's demands and their own rebellious constitutions is likewise greater.

The substance of the conflict at this stage suggests three questions. (1) What is the task laid upon the individual by the demands of this stage? (2) Does the "legitimate" sexual satisfaction compensate in a reasonable degree for the abstention in other directions? (3) What is the relation between any possible harmful effects of this abstention and the benefit to civilization?

Sexual Abstinence

The first question raises a problem which has often been discussed—the problem of sexual abstinence. The standard set by our civilization is that both sexes should abstain until marriage, and that individuals who are not legally married should abstain all their life long. The moral authorities, e.g. the churches, maintain that sexual abstinence is not injurious to the individual nor even difficult to compass. This view has also obtained a good deal of support from the medical profession. To master such a powerful impulse as the sexual instinct may well require all a person's energies. The form of mastery called sublimation, whereby the sexual energy is diverted to non-sexual cultural purposes, is only successful with a minority of people and then only intermittently. It is most difficult to carry out at the period when it is most required, namely during the passionate period of youth. Those who fail altogether to sublimate become in most cases neurotic or otherwise come to grief. The verdict of experience is that the majority in our society are constitutionally incapable of the heroic standard of abstinence which it sets. Those who would have fallen ill even under moderate restrictions fall ill earlier and more severely under the demands of our present civilized morality. Where there is any faulty predisposition or the course of development has been upset, no better safeguard against abnormality is known than sexual satisfaction itself. The stronger the disposition to neurosis the less tolerable is abstinence. For the component impulses already described become uncontrollable in proportion as they have been excluded from development. But even people who could have complied with the demands of the second stage of civilization and still kept their health will in many cases fall a victim to neurosis in the third stage, for the psychical value of sexual satisfaction increases with privation. It is as though the thwarted libido set about spying out weak spots in the structure of sexual life (and weak spots are seldom wanting) so as to break through somewhere or other as a neurotic substitute gratification in the form of a morbid symptom. The more we unearth the causes underlying nervous disorders the more convinced we become that their frequency in our society as compared with simpler societies originates in the stricter regulation of sexual activity.

Marriage

This brings us to our second question. Can sexual intercourse in legitimate marriage compensate fully for abstinence before marriage? A survey of modern life quickly produces an abundance of evidence pointing to a negative answer. The strictest form of our civilized sexual morality not only forbids intercourse with anyone but the marriage partner, but goes further and compels the couple to restrict their intercourse as a rule to a relatively small number of acts leading to conception. In addition there is, of course, the abstention for intervals required on hygienic grounds by the woman's state of health. Even where contraceptives are used there are serious difficulties, since all the devices so far available reduce enjoyment, disturb the finer susceptibilities of both partners, or even promote illness. Anxiety over the consequences of intercourse tends to dissipate the physical tenderness between the married couple, and very often at a later date dissipates the more tranquil love between them which should have followed the initial tempestuous passion. The result of all these factors in a sadly large number of cases is that marriage ceases after a few years to give the satisfaction of the sexual needs which it promised. Psychical deprivation and disappointment leave both partners reduced to their pre-conjugal condition, but poorer by the loss of an illusion. Once more they are driven back to their determination to restrain and side-track their sexual instinct. How far a man in mature years succeeds in doing so varies very much from one individual to another. Very often he begins reluctantly and furtively to take advantage of that margin of freedom which is tolerated by even the strictest code. The double code—one for men and another for women—which our society tacitly allows is the clearest possible admission that it does not believe in the possibility of fully obeying its own standards. And what of the position of women who, much more than men, are the guardians of the sexual interests of the race? Experience shows that they have only a limited capacity for sublimation. They may find a substitute object of love in their baby, but as the child grows he becomes less and less satisfactory in this rôle. Many women are condemned by the disappointments of marriage to severe life-long neurosis. Under our current cultural standard marriage has long ceased to be a panacea for the nervous disorders of women. The doctor may still recommend matrimony in such cases, but he ought to know that a girl must be very healthy if she is to stand modern marriage. At the same time he will be earnestly advising his male patients not to marry a girl who has been neurotic. It is possible that unfaithfulness would be a cure for the neurosis resulting from the disappointments of marriage. But the more strictly a wife has been brought up to accept the demands of civilization the more does she fear this way of escape. Conflict between her desires and her sense of duty will only drive her again to seek refuge in neurosis, for nothing protects her virtue so securely as illness.

Authorized marriage, to which the youth of civilized peoples are directed as a solution of their sexual problems, thus proves inadequate. It fails alike to compensate for the earlier abstention and to meet the demands of later life.

Our third question challenged us to balance the harmful effects of civilized sexual morality against the benefits which accrue to civilization from it. It is possible to admit the harmful effects but to regard the cultural gains as outweighing them. After all, it may be said, the more striking manifestations of these evils only appear in a minority of people. Freud confessed himself unable to balance the gain and loss at all precisely. He pointed out, however, that on the loss side a good deal more should be included than the neuroses and that the neuroses themselves are more significant than might commonly be thought.

In our civilization education aims at holding back sexual development and delaying sexual activity. This is certainly no harm to begin with. It may even be considered necessary in view of the late age at which members of the more educated classes attain independence and begin to earn their own living. The customs and institutions of our civilization, it should be remembered, are intimately related to one another and it is difficult to single out one of them for alteration regardless of the whole. But even in the most highly educated classes we cannot take it for granted that a young man will benefit from abstinence continued much beyond his twentieth year. Even if it does not make a neurotic of him it may have other harmful consequences. It may be true for some specially constituted natures that, as is often alleged, the struggle against such powerful instincts and the resulting reinforcement of ethical and æsthetic tendencies "steels" the character. It may also be true that it is the abstention from early sexual activity that makes possible the wide variations of individual character which are a prominent feature of civilized peoples. But in by far the greater number of cases the struggle against sexuality involves a great drain on the energy of the character, and it does this at the very time when a young man needs all his powers to gain a footing in the adult world and to win his share of its material goods. The balance between possible sublimation and indispensable sexual activity varies, of course, from one person to another. It varies, too, with different occupations. An abstinent artist is scarcely conceivable. An abstinent young intellectual is not a rarity. The young intellectual finds that abstinence increases his ability to concentrate. The work of the artist is probably stimulated to a considerable extent by his sexual experience. On the whole there does not seem to be much reason for thinking that sexual abstinence is a factor in producing confident and energetic men of action, or original thinkers, or bold pioneers and reformers. Far more often it produces " good " weaklings, who then become lost in the crowd which does its best to follow the initiative of strong characters.

The sexual instinct is notoriously persistent and unruly, and these characteristics crop up in the results produced by the attempt to abstain. The aim of education is not to suppress sexuality entirely but to suppress it up to the time of marriage. The idea is that it may then be given free rein because it serves a purpose that is approved of. In attempting this, education is taking on a difficult job. Moderate measures for repressing an instinct are less successful than extreme measures. The measures actually taken are only too likely to overdo the repression. The unwished-for result is that when the sexual instinct is in due course set free it is permanently impaired. This is the reason why total abstinence during youth is often not the best way of preparing a young man for marriage. Women seem to sense this and tend to prefer those of their suitors who have already proved themselves men with other women. In the case of women the harmful consequences of the strict demand for abstinence before marriage are particularly apparent. In our society education employs the most drastic measures to suppress the girl's sensuality until marriage. It not only forbids sexual intercourse and places a high value on the preservation of chastity, but it also tries to shield the growing young woman from temptation by keeping her in ignorance of the exact rôle she is later expected to play. It of course tolerates no love impulse which cannot lead to marriage. When this regime is in full authority the girl is one day suddenly allowed by her parents to fall in love. She cannot do so and enters upon marriage uncertain of her own feelings. This in turn means disappointment for the husband, who has stored up all his desires for the wife of his choice. Thanks to the artificial retarding of her development the girl is still attached to her parents. It was their authority which brought about the suppression of the sexual feeling, and psychically she has not got away from them. Physically she is frigid and the result is that her husband finds little enjoyment in his relations with her. Our civilized education goes out of its way to cultivate this type of woman, described by Freud as the " anæsthetic " type. These women conceive without pleasure and show little willingness to endure further childbirths after the painful experience of the first. Their education before marriage thus directly frustrates the very

Frigidity

purpose of marriage. Later on the wife may make good the retarded development and during the climax of her life the full power to love may awaken in her. But by then her relation to her husband has long been undermined and she is left with a choice between unsatisfied desire, infidelity, and neurosis.

This type of woman is certainly to be found in our modern civilization. Whether she is also found outside its range is a matter for investigation. Freud thought it probable that she would be found outside our civilization.

Sexual Behaviour and Character

Although sexual life is only part of the life of a human being a man or woman's behaviour in sexual matters is not a thing apart from his or her other modes of reaction to life. Indeed it is often a prototype for the whole of them. The man who shows determination in gaining possession of his love-object is likely to show a similar determination towards other aims. The man who abstains from satisfying a strong sexual instinct, will in other paths of life be resigned and conciliatory rather than energetic and active. This general truth that an individual's sexual behaviour is typical of his behaviour in other respects has an interesting particular application in the case of women. Women's training expressly discourages them from busying their minds with sex. A girl is naturally as inquisitive as a boy about this absorbing matter. But everything is done to head her off it. Any such curiosity is denounced as unwomanly and a sign of immoral tendencies. This policy has intimidated women from trying to find out not only about sex, but about other subjects as well. In the past at any rate it discouraged them from all mental effort and set up a depreciation of knowledge in general in their eyes. The extension of the prohibition beyond the sphere of sex takes place partly automatically and partly through associations. It works in the same way as the prohibition of religious speculation does or the taboo which prevents loyal subjects entertaining any thought which is out of harmony with their loyalty. Freud held that the inhibition of thought in the interests of sexual suppression is the real source of the intellectual inferiority of so many women. He rejected the theory of Moebius that the biological contrast between intellectual work and sexual activity was the cause of a " physiological mental weakness " in women.

Prohibition of Thought

Masturbation

It is often forgotten that abstention from intercourse with the opposite sex is not the same thing as abstention from all sexual activity. Successful abstinence is sometimes claimed by men who have only been able to forgo intercourse because they found satisfaction in masturbation or other similar activities connected with the auto-erotism of early childhood. They have no cause to congratulate themselves so heartily. This very connection makes these substitute activities by no means innocuous. Because they represent a regression to infantile forms of sexual life, they predispose to neurosis and psychosis. Furthermore, it is not as though masturbation were in line with the ideal standards of civilized sexual morality. It is, on the contrary, frowned upon. The young man who practises it, therefore, finds himself once again in conflict with the ideals of his education. Worse still, this form of indulgence undermines his character in a number of ways. First, because his discovery of a lazy way of attaining aims which properly require energy and effort will extend from his attitude to sex till it embraces his whole attitude to life. Secondly, because in the fantasies with which his imagination accompanies the indulgence the sexual object is exalted to a degree which is seldom to be reproduced in reality. (The witty Viennese writer, Karl Kraus, expressed this truth paradoxically in his cynical remark : " Coitus is merely an unsatisfactory substitute for masturbation.")

The main point of abstinence has, under stress of the exacting standard demanded by civilization and the severe task of making it effective, come to be the avoidance of the genital union of the sexes. So long as that union is avoided other forms of sexual activity will pass muster. The upshot has been to favour abstinence and substitute activities, both of which may be regarded as forms of obedience by halves. The so-called perverse forms of intercourse between the sexes, in which the rôle of the genitals is taken by other parts of the body, have acquired an enhanced social significance thanks to the remorseless taboo placed on normal intercourse in the name of morality. They are also of practical concern to society on hygienic grounds because of the possibility of infection. But from no point of view can they be regarded as harmless—in the way that similar irregularities are harmless when they are interwoven with a normal love intercourse as foreplay and auxiliary acts. These perversions are ethically reprehensible because they degrade the love relationship of two human beings from a serious matter to an indolent pastime involving neither risk nor spiritual participation. The spread of the homosexual forms of gratification is a symptom of the obstacles which have been put in the way of a normal sexual life. Some individuals are constitutionally homosexual and some become so through fixation in childhood, but there are in addition many others who have taken to homosexuality in adult life because of the check on the main stream of the libido.

The insistence on abstinence was never intended to bring about any such consequences as these. Yet these consequences follow relentlessly from it. And they strike at the roots of the very thing civilized sexual morality was concerned to sustain. That morality intended marriage to be the sole heir of all sexual tendencies. The consequences of its insistence on abstinence make preparation for marriage a very precarious matter. All those men who have become accustomed to types of sexual satisfaction other than the normal, through masturbation or perverse practices, develop in marriage a diminished potency. And all those women who could only preserve their virginity by similar means show themselves unresponsive to normal intercourse in marriage. With the capacity to love impaired in both husband and wife a marriage goes to pieces. Thanks to the man's diminished potency the woman will obtain no satisfaction and will remain frigid, whereas a powerful sexual experience might have enabled her to overcome the frigidity derived from her education. To add to their difficulties the man's diminished potency makes the use of contraceptives incompatible with satisfying intercourse. In their perplexity the couple come to regard sexual intercourse as the source of all difficulties and soon give it up. And with that they abandon the fundamental condition of married life.

To a layman the various conditions which have been described in the last few pages may seem exaggerated. Any doctor who has received the confidence of many married couples will acknowledge that situations of these various kinds are tragically common. Freud writes: "The uninitiated can hardly believe how rarely normal potency is to be found in the men, and how often frigidity in the women, among married couples living under the sway of our civilized sexual morality; what a degree of renunciation, often for both partners, is associated with marriage; and how little the marriage brings of the happiness that was so ardently desired."

The most obvious way of escape is neurosis. But the husband and wife are not the only people concerned. Such a marriage has a powerful and increasing effect on the child, or the limited number of children, whom it brings into the world. The child's disorders when they in their turn come to be dealt with may look at first sight like an inherited condition. But closer examination discloses the effects of strong infantile impressions. The mother, unsatisfied by her husband and neurotic, is over-tender and over-anxious towards the child. She has transferred to it her need for love and thus aroused in it sexual precosity. The child becomes aware of the unhappy relationship between its parents. This stimulates its emotional life so that, while still in its infancy, it experiences love, hate, and jealousy in their intensity. Strict training adds its force to the mechanisms of suppression, and so there is already at this early age a conflict which has within it all the elements needed to cause life-long neurosis.

Neuroses The full significance of neuroses is seldom reckoned with. Relatives dismiss them as of no consequence. Doctors may prescribe a few months' rest and convalescence. Both judgments amount to nothing much more than a form of speech designed to afford the sufferer a short-lived consolation. But a chronic neurosis, even if it does not completely paralyse the sufferer's existence, is as heavy a handicap to him in life as tuberculosis or a serious affection of the heart. This might be tolerated if neurotic illnesses merely cut off from the activity of the community a number of individuals who were in any case infirm and let the remainder play their part at the cost of a few disabilities affecting no one but themselves. But this is not so. And here lies the importance of the insufficient appreciation of these states. Neuroses, in proportion to their extent, always succeed in thwarting the social purpose: they actually do the work of the psychical forces which, because they are hostile to society, have been suppressed. The exorbitant demands of civilized society are paid for by the increase of neuroses. But society gains nothing by the transaction. Take the case—a not uncommon one—of a woman who does not love her husband, because neither the consummation of her marriage nor the experience of her married life has given her cause to love him. She longs to love him because that alone would realize the ideal of marriage to which she has been brought up. What does she do? She suppresses every impulse which would bring her true feelings to light and contradict her efforts to realize her ideal. She takes enormous trouble to play the part of a loving, tender, and submissive wife. And the result of this suppression of her true feelings will be a neurotic illness and in a short time her neurosis will take its revenge on her unloved husband by causing him precisely as much discontent and trouble as would have arisen from a simple acknowledgment of the true state of affairs. This example is typical of what neurosis can do. The socially inimical impulses whose suppression leads to a miscarriage of compensation need not be directly sexual. The same sort of thing can happen, for instance, to a man who suppresses a constitutional tendency to harshness and cruelty and becomes instead excessively " kind-hearted ". In doing so he often loses so much energy that he fails to achieve the full measure of his compensatory impulses and does rather less good on the whole than he would have done without suppression.

Anxiety There is another point which may be mentioned here. Hand in hand with the restriction of sexual activity in any community goes an increase of anxiety concerning life and an increase of the fear of death. These react on the individual's capacity for enjoyment and diminish his readiness to incur the risk of death even in the service of a cause. There is in people of this type a diminished inclination to beget children so that they deprive themselves of any share in the future.

In the light of all these consequences we may well raise the question whether our civilized sexual morality is worth the sacrifice it demands from us. We may be all the more inclined to ask this question if we are still so imperfectly purged of hedonism as to think that some degree of individual happiness should be among the aims of our cultural development.

ANXIETY [1]

Anxiety is something that everyone has experienced at some time or other. Most nervous people complain of it and describe it as their most terrible burden. What is it?

In the first place it is something that is felt—what psychologists call an "affective" condition (although we do not know what an affect is). In the second place it has, in a very high degree, the quality which is the opposite of pleasure. In the absence of any convenient word for this quality it has been called "unpleasure". But there are other feelings and sensations which are marked by a high degree of unpleasure, such as grief or tension or pain. What other distinctive characteristics has anxiety to make it so easily distinguishable among the whole range of unpleasurable affects?

General Characteristics

Two or three points stand out at once. Everyone would agree that the unpleasurable quality of anxiety has a special flavour of its own, though this is difficult to identify and name. In addition anxiety is accompanied by fairly definite physical sensations which we can refer to particular organs of the body. For example, there are often very clear physical sensations connected with the heart and the breathing apparatus. These indicate that motor innervations, i.e. processes of discharge, play a part in the general phenomenon of anxiety.

We have, therefore, picked out three points which characterize states of anxiety: (1) a specific quality of unpleasure, (2) acts of discharge, and (3) perceptions of these acts. The second and third points mark at once a difference between anxiety and such similar conditions as grief and pain. The latter have no motor manifestations or, if they have, they are not an integral part of the condition but a result of it or a reaction to it.

On general grounds we should be disposed to conclude that anxiety has its foundations in an increase of excitation, which produces the quality of unpleasure on the one hand, and on the other finds relief through acts of discharge along particular channels. That would be a physiological account of the matter. For our purposes it is not enough. As psychologists we should be inclined to say that there must be a factor belonging to the individual's own history which links together the sensations of

[1] Inhibitions, Symptoms, and Anxiety, pp. 96–112, 158–165.

anxiety and its innervations. In other words, we should expect an anxiety state to be the reproduction of some experience which contains the necessary conditions for an increase of excitation and a discharge along particular channels. We should be inclined, further, to say that it is from this circumstance that the unpleasure gets its specific quality. In human beings the prototype of experiences which would fit this bill is birth. The child's separation from his mother's body is the first great shock in life. Freud is, therefore, inclined to regard anxiety states as a reproduction of the trauma of birth. And that experience, he says, " involves just such a concatenation of painful feelings, of discharges of excitation, and of bodily sensations, as to have become a prototype for all occasions on which life is endangered, ever after to be reproduced again in us as the dread or ' anxiety ' condition."

Affects

This does not imply that anxiety occupies a different position from all other affective conditions. Freud thought that the other affects are also reproductions of very early experiences of vital importance—perhaps even pre-individual experiences. He was inclined to regard them as " universal, typical, and innate hysterical attacks, comparable with the recently and individually acquired attacks which occur in hysterical neuroses and whose origin and significance as memory symbols have been revealed by analysis ". This surmise, he admitted, remained to be demonstrated.

Objections may be raised to the view that anxiety goes back to birth. It may be argued that anxiety is a reaction which is probably common to all organisms, and certainly to all organisms of a higher order, whereas birth is only experienced by mammals. It may be questioned, too, whether for all mammals birth amounts to a trauma. Therefore, it would be argued, there can be anxiety without the prototype of birth. In reply to this objection Freud urges that since anxiety has an indispensable function to fulfil as a reaction to danger, it may well have a different pattern in different organisms. We do not know whether anxiety in animals far removed from man involves the same sensations and innervations as it does in man himself. What happens in the case of other creatures is no argument against the view that in man anxiety is modelled on the shock experience of birth.

Function of Anxiety

There seems no doubt that anxiety has its function as a reaction to danger and that it is reproduced whenever a situation of danger occurs. This raises further considerations. The innervations involved in the original state of anxiety probably had a perfectly good meaning and purpose. In the same way the muscular movements which accompany a first hysterical attack form part of an action appropriate to the particular situation of the attack. Thus in birth the innervations directed to the breathing apparatus probably prepare the way for the activity of the lungs, and the accelerated heart-beat helps to keep the blood free from toxic substances. Later on they are repeated in anxiety states where they have no such appropriateness, just as muscular movements are reproduced in repetitions of a hysterical attack. In a new situation of danger it may well be quite unsuitable for the individual to respond with the anxiety state which was his reaction to an earlier danger. A new reaction of a different kind might be much more appropriate. But his behaviour may still be useful if he recognizes the situation of danger before it actually overtakes him—if, that is to say, an outbreak of anxiety becomes a danger signal. He can then get rid of his anxiety in time by taking more suitable measures. Anxiety can therefore emerge in two ways : inexpedient if a new danger situation has actually occurred, or expedient if it gives a danger signal and prevents the new situation from occurring.

Anxiety as Danger Signal

We have spoken rather glibly of " danger ". What is a danger ? In the process of birth there is a real danger to life—an objective danger. But the child who is being born has no knowledge that its existence is in actual danger of being terminated. It can only be aware of some vast upheaval which disturbs the economy of its narcissistic libido. Great quantities of excitation crowd in upon it and give rise to new sensations of unpleasure. Many of its organs become charged with a great increase of energy. Now what in all this can we identify as distinctive of a danger situation ?

Infantile Anxiety

We have no idea of what the whole experience means psychologically to the baby ; far too little is known about the mental make-up of a new-born child. We cannot be certain that even the description given in the preceding paragraph is a correct statement of the child's point of view. It is easy to say that anxiety will be repeated in every situation which recalls the event of birth. The important thing to know is what it is that recalls that event and what it is in that event that is recalled.

Freud came to the conclusion that the earliest phobias of infancy could not be traced back directly to impressions of birth. They were unexplained. Undoubtedly there is in the child a certain preparedness for anxiety. But this preparedness is not at its height immediately after birth, thereafter decreasing slowly as time goes by. It does not emerge till later on as the infant's mental development takes its course. It lasts for a certain period of childhood. If the early phobias continue beyond that period there is reason to suspect a neurotic disturbance, although it is by no means clear what their relation is to the neuroses that occur in later childhood.

The forms of anxiety which children exhibit are various and only a few of them are understandable to adults. We must confine ourselves to these. There is the well-known example of the child in the dark. There are signs of anxiety when a child is alone or left with an unknown person instead of its mother or someone else to whom it is accustomed. One condition is common to all three of these examples : the child misses someone who is loved and longed for. This seems to offer us a clue to the nature of anxiety and a hope of reconciling the contradictions that seem to surround it. The child pictures the person longed for. The picture is no doubt intense, perhaps even in a hallucinatory way at first. But the child finds that picturing the beloved person does not bring that person any nearer. The longing now seems to turn into anxiety and the anxiety has all the appearance of expressing the child's perplexity. It does not know what to do or how to cope with the intensity of its longing. In fact the anxiety appears to be a reaction to the felt loss of the loved object. This aspect reminds us at once that the earliest anxiety of all—the anxiety of birth—occurs at separation from the mother, and that the castration anxiety of later on is also a fear of being separated from a highly valued object.

But why does the infant want to perceive the presence of its mother? Because it knows by experience that the mother gratifies all its needs and gratifies them promptly. The situation which to the child spells danger and against which it wants to be safeguarded is thus a situation of non-gratification. It is characterized by a growing tension, due to need, and a helplessness in the face of it. If we adopt this view it is possible to fit all the facts together. We have a situation of non-gratification in which stimulation rises to a disagreeable height and the infant is unable to master it or discharge it psychologically. For the infant this must be analogous to the experience of being born. It is thus a repetition of that situation of danger. The two situations have in common a disturbance of the child's economy, caused by the accumulation of quantities of stimulation which require to be disposed of. This common element is the essence of the " danger ", and in both cases the reaction is the same—anxiety. There is no need to suppose that the infant carries with it anything more from the experience of birth than this way of indicating the presence of danger. We may notice, by the way, that the anxiety reaction is still appropriate and useful at the sucking stage, because its discharge into the breathing and vocal apparatus now serves the purpose of summoning the mother.

As the child discovers by experience that an outside object—its mother, whom it can see—can terminate the dangerous situation reminiscent of birth, the nature of what it fears shifts. It is displaced from the situation to the condition which determined that situation, namely the absence of the mother. That is now the danger. And as soon as that danger arises the child gives the signal of anxiety, before stimulation has accumulated to create the original dreaded situation. Once the child has taken this step it has made important progress in the provision for its own self-preservation. At the same time it has taken the step from the automatic and involuntary new-creation of anxiety to the intentional reproduction of anxiety as a danger signal.

Anxiety as an automatic phenomenon and as a danger signal is a product of the mental helplessness which is a natural counterpart of the infant's biological helplessness. The fact that, in both the new-born baby and the infant in arms, anxiety depends on separation from the mother calls for no special explanation. Before birth the mother satisfied all the needs of the fœtus from her own body. After birth she continues to do so, though partly through other means. There is a much greater continuity between life in the womb and the first stages of infancy than we might be inclined to believe. The child's biological situation as a fœtus is replaced by a psychological relation to its mother. The mother is now an object for the child, which she was not while it was still in the womb; at that time there were no objects at all.

If this account is correct it obviously leaves no room for any theory of the abreaction of the birth trauma. The only function of anxiety that is left is the function of signalling the approach of a situation of danger.

Fear and Anxiety

We have not finished yet with the characteristics of anxiety as an affective condition. Anxiety has undoubtedly some affinity with expectation. It has a quality of indefiniteness and lack of object. If the feeling has found an object we use the word " fear " rather than " anxiety ". Yet anxiety is *about* something. Another point : why are not all reactions of anxiety neurotic ? Why do we regard so many of them as perfectly normal ? And finally, what is the difference between objective anxiety and neurotic anxiety ? An examination of these problems may throw some further light on the subject.

To begin with the last problem. We have gone behind reactions of anxiety to situations of danger. We saw that what are psychologically danger situations are not necessarily situations of objective danger. Objective danger is a danger that is known. Anxiety about a known danger of this kind may be called " objective anxiety "—as distinct from neurotic anxiety which is anxiety about an unknown danger. Neurotic danger is thus a danger that has still to be discovered. Analysis has shown that it is an instinctual danger. What the analyst does is to bring this danger, which was not known till then, into consciousness. He thus makes neurotic anxiety no different from objective anxiety, so that it can be dealt with in the same way.

Neurotic Anxiety

There are two ways of reacting to objective danger. One is anxiety—an affective reaction. The other is to take protective action. As we have seen the two may co-operate usefully when the one gives the signal for the other. They can also behave in a useless or harmful way, when the anxiety overruns and paralyses protective action.

Objective anxiety and neurotic anxiety do not always keep their distance. A mixing of their characteristics is also possible, as when the danger is objective but the anxiety is greater than seems warranted. It is this excess of anxiety which reveals the presence of a neurotic element. Such cases always show on analysis that an unknown instinctual danger has attached itself to the known objective danger.

What is the essence and meaning of a danger situation ? Obviously it consists in a person's estimation of his own powers compared to the magnitude of the danger, and his admission of helplessness in the face of it. The helplessness is physical if the danger is objective, psychological if the danger is instinctual.

His estimate will be guided by his own past experiences and whether that estimate is right or wrong is for our purpose immaterial. If he has in the past actually experienced a situation of helplessness of this kind it will have left its mark. Freud calls this a "traumatic situation". There is good reason to distinguish between a traumatic situation and a danger situation.

Traumatic Situations

Self-preservation is an aim which calls for ability on the individual's own part. The individual has made an important advance in developing that ability if he can foresee a traumatic situation entailing helplessness and so take appropriate steps, instead of simply waiting for it to overtake him. A danger situation contains reason for this expectation. The signal of anxiety now plays its part by announcing that a situation of helplessness is likely to set in. In other words it says: "This situation reminds me of a traumatic experience I have had before. I will therefore anticipate the trauma and behave as though it had already come, while there is yet time to turn it aside." Anxiety is thus both an expectation of a trauma and a repetition of it in a modified and more manageable form. The two characteristics of anxiety which we noted earlier have thus a different origin. Its affinity with expectation comes from the danger situation. Its indefiniteness and lack of object belong to the traumatic situation of helplessness which is anticipated.

Let us summarize what we have been saying about this sequence: anxiety—danger—helplessness (trauma). A danger situation is a recognized, remembered, and expected situation of helplessness. Anxiety is the original reaction to helplessness and is reproduced subsequently in the danger situation as a signal. The ego, which underwent the original trauma passively, now repeats it actively in a modified version in the hope of being able to master it. Children do this systematically with the painful impressions they receive by reproducing them in their play. They were passive victims the first time; this time by repeating the experience actively they hope to master it psychologically. But the decisive step is the displacement of the anxiety reaction from its origin in the situation of helplessness to the expectation of that situation. After that come the later displacements, from the danger to the condition occasioning the danger—the loss of the mother or other object and the modifications of that loss that we have already seen.

Spoiling of Children If a small child is spoilt the unfortunate result is that the danger of losing the object which is a protection against situations of helplessness grows to a disproportionate importance compared with every other danger. It therefore encourages the individual to remain in the state of childhood with its characteristic physical and mental helplessness.

To return to our distinction between objective anxiety and neurotic anxiety. An objective danger, as we saw, threatens the individual from outside, while a neurotic danger threatens him with an instinctual demand. We have seen, too, that the reason for the apparently intimate connection between anxiety and neurosis is that the ego defends itself against an instinctual danger with the aid of the anxiety reaction in the same way as it does against an objective danger, but that this line of defence ends in neurosis because of an imperfection of the psychological apparatus. We have seen, further, that an instinctual demand often becomes a danger—an internal danger—because to gratify it would be to invite an external danger.

Instinctive Anxiety? If an internal danger may represent an external one it is also true that an external danger must have become internalized in some way if it is to have significance for the ego. It must have been seen as related to some situation of helplessness already experienced by the individual. Unlike animals man seems to have been endowed with little or no instinctive recognition of the external dangers around him. Small children are liable to do hair-raising things which put their very lives in danger. That is the very reason why they must have protection from another person. With regard to the traumatic situation in which the individual is helpless there is a convergence of external and internal dangers, a point where instinctual demands and objective dangers meet. The economic situation is the same whether the trouble be a pain which will not stop or a pressure of instinctual needs which cannot obtain gratification. The motor helplessness finds expression in psychological helplessness.

Phobias This brings up again the riddle of phobias in early childhood. We already considered three examples which are comprehensible as reactions to the danger of losing the beloved object. There are others, such as the fear of small animals and thunderstorms, which might possibly be the vestiges of that inborn readiness to meet objective dangers which is so strongly developed in other animals. In man the only appropriate part of this ancient inheritance is that which refers to the loss of the love-object. If childhood phobias become fixated and carry over into adult life, analysis shows that their original content has got associated with instinctual demands so that it has come to represent internal as well as external dangers.

The content of the danger situation is naturally influenced by the child's growth and development. Its increasing independence, the differentiation of its mental equipment, the advent of new needs, all have their effect. We have already studied the change of content from the loss of the mother as an object to castration. A further change comes about through the influence of the super-ego. The parent from whom castration was feared is succeeded as moral authority by an impersonal institution, and with this change the danger becomes less clearly defined. Castration anxiety is transformed into moral or social anxiety and it is then more difficult to say what the anxiety is about. The threat of separation and expulsion from the horde only applies to the later portion of the super-ego, formed under the influence of social prototypes. It does not apply at the outset when the super-ego corresponds to the introjected parental authority. What now appears as the danger and evokes an anxiety signal is the prospect that the super-ego will be angry or withdraw its love or inflict punishment. The final stage which fear of the super-ego reaches is the fear of death—in other words, fear for life. This is a projection of fear of the super-ego on to the powers that rule the Universe, on to destiny or fate.

IDENTIFICATION[1]

The earliest way in which an emotional tie with another person is expressed is identification. We have seen it already in the early history of the Oedipus complex, when the little boy desires to grow like his father, be like his father, and take his father's place everywhere. The common phrase for this is that the boy takes his father as his ideal. There is nothing in this of a passive or feminine attitude towards the father or towards males in general. It is typically masculine and helps to prepare the way for the Oedipus complex.

Ideals

Simultaneously with this identification with his father, or a little later, the boy begins to develop a straightforward sexual attachment to his mother. He has thus two psychologically distinct ties, which continue side by side for some time without influencing or interfering with each other. But the course of development is towards a unification of mental life and so at last they converge. From this convergence originates the normal Oedipus complex. The boy's identification with his father takes on a hostile colouring. He wishes to replace his father in regard to his mother. In fact identification is ambivalent from the start: it can turn into an expression of tenderness or it can turn into a desire for someone's removal. It behaves as though it were derived from the first, the oral, phase of the development of the libido, in which the object that we desire and value is destroyed in the process of assimilation. The cannibal, with his devouring affection for his enemies, has remained at this standpoint.

Ambivalence of Identification

What happens to this identification with the father after the Oedipus complex has come into operation? Its later history may easily be lost from view. If the Oedipus complex becomes inverted, the father becomes the object of a feminine attitude, an object to which the sexual instincts look for satisfaction. In that case the son's identification with the father has become the forerunner of an object tie with the father. The same holds good, *mutatis mutandis*, of a daughter as well.

Identification and Choice of Object

The distinction between identification with the father and choice of the father as an object is easily stated. It is the difference between to be and to have. In the first case the father is what one

[1] Group Psychology and the Analysis of the Ego, pp. 60–80.

would like to be; in the second, what one would like to have. It depends on whether the tie is to the subject or to the object of the ego. The former is possible before ever any choice of sexual object has been made. Its effect is an attempt to mould the ego on the pattern of the one taken as a model.

Neurotic Identification

Identification can occur as part of the structure of a neurotic symptom. Let us try to disentangle it from its complicated connections. Suppose that a little girl develops the same symptoms as her mother, e.g. a tormenting cough. This may come about in several different ways. It may be an identification arising from the Oedipus complex and signifying a hostile desire to take the mother's place. The symptom is an expression of her object love for her father. Under the influence of a feeling of guilt she is being shown her own desire to replace her mother. What the symptom is saying is: "You wanted to be your mother. Very well, then, now you are —anyhow as far as the pain goes." This is the mechanism behind a hysterical symptom. On the other hand the symptom may be the same as that of the person who is loved, e.g. if it had been the father who had a cough. In that case identification would have appeared instead of object choice, and object choice would have regressed to identification. Identification, as was pointed out already, is the earliest and original form of emotional tie. It often happens that where there is repression and where the mechanisms of the unconscious are dominant, object choice regresses to identification. In other words, the ego takes on characteristics that belong to the object. We have seen that in these identifications the person copied is sometimes the one who is loved and sometimes the one who is not. In both cases the identification is a limited one: only a single characteristic is borrowed.

Hysterical Identification

A third and important type of symptom formation is particularly frequent. It is one which leaves out of account any object relation to the person copied. Here is an example. One of the girls at a boarding school receives a letter from someone with whom she is secretly in love. The contents of the letter arouse her jealousy. She reacts with a fit of hysterics. Some of her friends who know about it then proceed to have fits of hysterics, too, although none of them is in love with the writer of the letter. The mechanism is one of identification. It is based on the desire to put oneself in the same situation. The other girls would like to have a secret love affair too and under the influence of a sense of guilt they accept the distress which it would involve. They do not exhibit the symptom out of sympathy with the first girl. The sympathy only arises out of the identification, as may be seen by the fact that infection of this kind can take place in circumstances where there can be little or no previous sympathy. What happens is that one ego discovers a significant similarity with another ego on one point—a similar readiness for emotion, in our example. On this one point an identification is built, which is then displaced on to the symptom which the other ego has exhibited. Identification through the symptom marks a point of coincidence which has to be kept repressed.

Our findings about identification are three: (1) It is the original form of emotional tie with an object; (2) it may be a substitute for an object tie by way of regression; and (3) it may arise through perception of a quality shared with some other person who is not an object of the sexual instinct. In this third case the more important the common quality is the more successful the partial identification may become. It may indeed be the beginning of a new tie.

Identification and Group Formation

After what has been said it is natural to go on to the surmise that what binds members of a group together is in the nature of an identification, based on some important emotional quality which the members have in common. We may also suspect that this common quality is the nature of the tie with the leader. In fact we are far from having finished with identification. There is the problem raised by "empathy", that process of feeling our way into the thoughts and attitudes of other people, which plays the largest part in our understanding of what is inherently foreign to our own ego. What is its relation to identification?

Empathy

For our purposes here the immediate emotional effects of identification are sufficient. Its significance for our intellectual life must be left on one side. Psycho-analytic research has been able to show the part played by identification in some cases which are not immediately comprehensible. We shall consider two of these cases in detail.

Homosexuality

In a large number of cases male homosexuality originates in the following way. A young man has had an unusually long and intense attachment to his mother in the sense of the Oedipus complex. Eventually, when puberty has passed, it is time to find some other object for his libido. But the young man does not abandon his mother. Instead he identifies himself with her and now casts about for objects to replace his own ego. He wants to bestow on them the love and care which his mother bestowed on him. The sudden transformation is not the only striking feature of this identification. The scale of it is at least as striking, for it remoulds the ego in one of its most important aspects—its sexual character—on the model of what up till then has been the object. The object itself is given up entirely or relegated to the unconscious.

Introjection

Identification with an object that it renounced or lost, as a substitute for it—in other words, introjection of this object into the ego—is nothing new. Something of the kind has occasionally been observed in small children. There is the historic case of a child who was unhappy over the loss of a kitten, announced that he himself was now the kitten, went about on all fours, refused to eat at table, and so forth. Another instance of introjection of the object is provided by the analysis of melancholia. Among the most remarkable causes of melancholia is the real or emotional loss of a loved object. One of the main characteristics of these cases is a terrible self-depreciation accompanied by merciless self-criticism and self-reproaches. In the course of analysis it comes to light that the disparagement and reproaches are really directed at the lost object. The ego is taking its revenge upon the object, the object has been introjected into the ego and its shadow lies over the ego.

Melancholia

These cases of melancholia show us the ego divided against itself. It has fallen in two and one part rages against the other. The part which is being raged against is the one which has been altered by introjection to contain the lost object. The part which behaves so cruelly comprises the conscience and the critical function, which even in normal situations adopt a censorious attitude, though never so mercilessly and unjustifiably. Freud found himself compelled to postulate that some such critical faculty develops in our ego, which may separate itself from the rest of the ego and come into conflict with it. This faculty, sitting in judgment like a supreme court, he called the *ego ideal.* He ascribed to it the functions of self-observation, moral conscience, the censorship of dreams, and the chief rôle in repression. He described its history as follows: "It is the heir to the original narcissum in which

The Ego-ideal

the childish ego found its self-sufficiency ; it gradually gathers up from the influences of the environment the demands which that environment makes upon the ego and which the ego cannot always rise to ; so that a man, when he cannot be satisfied with the ego itself, may nevertheless be able to find satisfaction in the ego ideal which has been differentiated out of the ego." The ego ideal develops under the influence of superior powers and in particular of parents. It is therefore natural that the distance between the ego ideal and the real ego varies greatly from one person to another. With many people this differentiation within the ego remains at a childhood stage.

The pathological examples of homosexuality and melancholia which we have looked at do not exhaust the problems of identification. The riddle of group formation has been no more than touched upon. Any more adequate study would have to trace the path from identification by way of imitation to empathy. It would be necessary to investigate the mechanism by which we are enabled to take up any attitude at all towards the mental life of another person. But it is necessary to move on to another subject.

Love

The caprice of language gives the name of love to a great many kinds of emotional relationship. Then, again, as if in doubt as to what is real genuine love it hints at a whole scale of possibilities. The usage of language usually corresponds to some kind of reality and the psychologist has no difficulty in discovering many different kinds of love.

There is what is called common sensual love. The sexual instincts are directed towards an object with a view to obtaining direct sexual satisfaction. When this has been obtained the energy has all gone out of it. The situation, however, rarely remains quite as simple as this. The need which has been satisfied will revive, and this could be foreseen. The knowledge that it would return must have been the first motive for directing more than a transient attention to the sexual object and for " loving " it in the intervals between the outbursts of passion.

The astonishing course of development followed by the human being adds another factor. In his first phase a child finds the first object for his love in one or other of his parents. All of his sexual instincts have been concentrated upon this object. Repression then forces him to give up the majority of his infantile sexual aims. He is left with a deep mortification in his relation to his parents. He remains tied to them, but the instincts which tie him are inhibited as regards their aim. Henceforward the emotions which he feels towards his parents are " tender " not sensual. The earlier " sensual " tendencies disappear from his consciousness into the strong-room of the unconscious. At puberty new and very powerful tendencies set in whose aims are directly sexual. If circumstances are unfavourable they remain separate from the " tender " emotional trends which are already there. They form a sensual current on their own. A man of this kind displays a sentimental enthusiasm for women whom he profoundly respects, but who do not stir him to sexual desire, and he will only have intercourse with other women whom he does not " love " and may even despise. The usual development, however, is that the adolescent succeeds to some extent in uniting the heavenly love and the earthly love, and his relation to the object of his choice is marked by the interaction of unhibited instincts with instincts which are inhibited as regards their aim. The extent to which anyone is in love, as opposed to being sensually aroused, may be measured by the share taken by the instincts of tenderness.

Tenderness

Sexual Over-Estimation

Everyone has noticed that the love object (of other people) is over-estimated. It is to a considerable extent exempt from criticism and all its characteristics are more highly esteemed than those of people who are not loved or than its own were before the lover arrived. If the sensual tendencies are effectively repressed the illusion may be entertained that the object has come to be loved sensually on account of its spiritual merits. The fact may be that its sensual charm was what lent it these merits.

Idealization

This falsification of judgment is due to our tendency of idealization. As a matter of fact idealization makes it easier for us to find our way about. When we are in love a considerable quantity of narcissistic libido overflows on to the object of our love. It has often been noted that the person with whom a man or woman falls in love may serve as a substitute for some unattained ego ideal. We love it for perfections we have striven after ourselves and we now seek to obtain them in this roundabout way as a sop to our narcissism. If idealization can bring the love object nearer to this ideal so much the better.

If the young man falls deeper and deeper in love and carries the process of over-estimation still further, the picture becomes even clearer. The tendencies towards direct sexual satisfaction may be thrust entirely out of sight. This regularly happens with a young man's sentimental passion. The ego becomes more and more modest and retiring, the object more and more sublime, until at last it gains command of the entire self-love of the ego. The object has consumed the ego, as it were, which was only too glad to sacrifice itself. Of course, whenever anyone is in love there are signs of humility, of the limitation of narcissism, and of a disposition to self-injury. These are merely exaggerated in the extreme case till they remain in sole and undisputed possession.

This extreme course is the more likely to happen where love is unhappy and cannot be satisfied. For where sexual satisfaction is obtained there is always some reduction in the over-estimation of the object. In the case of unhappy love the devotion of the ego to the object is hardly distinguishable from a sublimated devotion to an abstract idea. With this development the function of the ego ideal simply ceases. The criticism which that faculty would normally exercise is in abeyance. The object can do nothing wrong. Conscience has no say in anything that is done for the object's sake ; in the blindness of love the lover is capable of committing crime " with a good conscience ". In short the object has taken the place of the ego ideal.

Infatuation Such excesses of being in love are generally called fascination or infatuation. There is a distinction between this and identification. In identification the ego has enriched itself with the properties of the object. In infatuation it has impoverished itself by surrendering itself to the object and putting the object in the place of its own most important component. As a distinction this is good enough. But a little closer consideration shows that an account of this kind creates an illusion of opposites which are unreal. There is no reality in the appearance of enrichment and impoverishment. It is a matter of taste whether we say that the infatuated ego has surrendered itself to the object or introjected the object into itself. Perhaps we can find another distinction which has more substance in it. In the case of identification the object has been lost or renounced and then set up again inside the ego, which makes a partial change in itself to approximate in one respect to the lost object. In the case of infatuation the object is anything but lost ; the ego charges it full of significance and at its own expense. But let us pause a moment. Are we quite sure that in identification all attachment to the object has been given up ? Can there be no identification combined with retention of the object ? This is a delicate question. Before we start discussing it let us consider whether there is not yet another alternative which may be nearer the truth of the matter. What is it that the object replaces—the ego or the ego ideal?

Hypnosis

From being in love to hypnosis is a short step. The points of agreement are obvious. There is the same humility, submission, and absence of criticism towards the hypnotist as there is towards the loved object. There is the same surrender of initiative. Obviously the hypnotist takes the place of the ego ideal. In hypnosis everything is even clearer and more accentuated, so that there would be more sense in using hypnosis to illuminate being in love than vice versa. The hypnotist is the sole object and the patient pays no attention to anyone else. The ego experiences his requests and assertions in a dreamlike fashion. Since the testing of the reality of things is one of the functions of the ego ideal it is not surprising that the ego will accept a perception as real if it is vouched for by the faculty (or its deputy) which ordinarily has the office of testing reality. The extreme clarity and unambiguousness of hypnotic phenomena is in part due to the complete absence of tendencies which are uninhibited in their sexual aims. In hypnosis the relation of the patient to the hypnotist is the devotion of someone in love to an unlimited degree, but with sexual satisfaction ruled out. In the case of being in love that satisfaction is only temporarily excluded and remains in the background as a possible later aim.

Hypnosis and Group Formation

There is another way of looking at the hypnotic relation. It is, in a sense, a group formation composed of two members. Group formation is a complicated fabric. What hypnosis does is to isolate from that fabric one element—the behaviour of the follower to the leader. It is distinguished from any ordinary group formation by its limitation in number, just as it is distinguished from being in love by the absence of direct sexual tendencies. From this point of view we may say that it has a position midway between the two.

We may notice that the sexual tendencies which produce such lasting ties between men are precisely those that are inhibited as regards their aims. The reason is simple. These are the tendencies which are incapable of complete satisfaction. That is why they last. The sexual tendencies which are uninhibited in regard to their aim suffer a marked reduction through the loss of energy every time the aim is achieved. It is the fate of sensual love to expire when it is satisfied. If it is to last it must have an admixture from the first of those purely tender components which are inhibited as regards their aims, or else it must itself be transformed in this way.

There is more in hypnosis, of course, than the formulation given a few lines back. There are features of it which are unexplained and mysterious, and it is this fact that prevents us from immediately seizing on hypnosis to solve the riddle of the libidinal constitution of groups. There is an element of paralysis derived from the relation between someone who has superior power and someone who is powerless. This aspect may be the link with the hypnosis of terror found in animals. It is by no means clear how hypnosis is produced. Its relationship to sleep is another problem. Then the peculiar way in which some people can resist it while others cannot points to some factor still unknown. It may be an unknown factor which accounts for the purity of the attitudes of the libido which hypnosis exhibits. It is well known that however complete the acquiescence of the patient may be in other respects, his moral conscience may refuse some suggestions. On the other hand this may be due to the fact that, as it is usually practised, some inkling may remain that what is taking place is only a game.

It is now possible to give the formula for the libidinal constitution of groups, or at least of those groups that have a leader and have not been led by too much organization to acquire secondarily the characteristics of an individual. Freud formulates it in these words: "A primary group of this kind is a number of individuals who have substituted one and the same object for their ego ideal and have consequently identified themselves with one another in their ego."

THE SUPER-EGO[1]

The Conscience

There is hardly any part of ourselves that we separate off from our ego or so easily set over against it as our conscience. Time and again a person refrains from something which looks like giving him pleasure on the ground that " his conscience will not allow it ". And if he is seduced by the expectation of pleasure into doing something which the voice of conscience has protested against, his conscience punishes him with its reproaches and makes him feel remorse for it.

We might be inclined to say that the function which we are trying to distinguish within the ego is the conscience and leave it at that. But it is more prudent to keep that function as a separate entity and assume that conscience is one of its activities. Another activity would be that self-observation which is the necessary preliminary to the judicial office of conscience. This function in the ego Freud calls the *super-ego.*

Freud was well aware that critics of his psychology of the ego might assert that he did no more than take everyday abstractions literally, magnify them, and then turn them from concepts into things. His answer was that anybody trying to study the psychology of the ego would find it difficult to avoid what was already familiar. It was not a question of making new discoveries, but of finding new ways of looking at things and of grouping the facts. He added that his efforts were all made against a background of the facts of pathology, a background missing in popular psychology.

This super-ego, to return, enjoys a certain independence, pursues its own ends, and is independent of the ego as regards the energy at its disposal. The facts of pathology at once show that in its relations with the ego all is not peaceful. We are faced with a clinical picture which throws into strong relief the severity and even cruelty of the super-ego. The condition of melancholia,

Melancholia

or more particularly the melancholic attack, illustrates this state of affairs. In this disease the most remarkable characteristic is the way in which the super-ego treats the ego. The melancholiac, during his periods of health, can be more or less severe towards himself, like anybody else. But when he has a melancholic attack his super-ego becomes

[1] New Introductory Lectures on Psycho-Analysis, pp. 81–91.

a veritable tartar. It abuses, maltreats, and humiliates the ego, threatens it with the direst punishments, reproaches it for long-forgotten actions which were regarded quite lightly at the time, and generally behaves as though it had spent its whole time drawing up a charge sheet and only waiting for its present access of strength to bring it forward and pass sentence. The super-ego has the ego at its mercy and applies to it the most exacting standards. It represents, in fact, the total demands of morality. Our moral sense of guilt is the expression of the tension between the ego and the super-ego. It is a very strange experience to observe the operations of the super-ego in a melancholiac. What we see is morality, supposedly planted deep in our hearts by the Creator, functioning as a periodical phenomenon. For after some months during which the melancholia has prevailed the whole moral fuss subsides. The censorious voice of the super-ego is still and the ego is reinstated into all the rights of a normal man until the next attack. In some forms of melancholia the intervals between the attacks are the occasion of complete abandonment. The ego gives itself up to triumph and ecstasy, as though the super-ego had been overthrown or merged with itself. This emancipated manic ego lets itself go in an uninhibited indulgence of all its desires.

"Morality as a Periodical Phenomenon"

Psycho-analysis has thrown a good deal of light on the formation of the super-ego and the origin of conscience. Kant once declared that two things filled his soul with ever new and ever growing awe—the starry heavens above us and the moral law within us. The stars are unquestionably superb, but the moral law within us is an uneven and doubtful partner for them, since many men have only a limited share of it, hardly enough to be worth mentioning. The view that conscience is of divine origin corresponds, if interpreted, with the findings of a naturalistic psychology. Conscience is no doubt something within us, but it has not been there from the beginning. In this respect it is the opposite of sexuality, which is present from the very beginning of life. Small children are notoriously a-moral. They have no inhibitions against their pleasure-seeking impulses. Such things only come later. The first restrictions upon them are imposed by the external authority of their parents. The child lives and grows under the all-embracing influence of the parents. They grant tokens of affection or withhold them. They threaten punishment which, in addition to

Kant's Saying

bearing feared on its own account, also means to the child the loss of love. This objective anxiety is the forerunner of the later moral anxiety, just as the parental authority is the forerunner of the later super-ego and of conscience. The second of these situations, which we are all too prone to regard as the normal state of affairs, only arises later on. The prohibitions come from outside to begin with. They are introjected, so that the super-ego develops to take the place of the parental authority. Once it is established it observes, guides, and threatens the ego in the same way as the parents did.

The Parental Authority

The super-ego, which thus succeeds the parental authority, is no mere legatee. It is the true-born heir. It proceeds directly from it and wields its power with the same aims and even the same methods. There is a difference, however, between the two. The super-ego seems to have made a one-sided selection, to have chosen only the severity and the preventive and punitive functions of the parents. Their loving care is not taken up and continued by it. It would be easy to understand this in the case of parents who really ruled with a rod of iron. But the odd thing is that the super-ego of the child may be just as harsh and unforgiving when the parents have been gentle and kind and avoided threats and punishment as far as possible.

The process by which the authority is transferred from the parents to the super-ego is complicated and imperfectly understood. Its basis is identification which, as we have seen, is the most primitive kind of emotional tie with another person. The establishment of the super-ego is a successful example of identification with the parental function. This creation of a superior function within the ego is closely bound up with the fate of the Oedipus complex. The super-ego is thus the heir of that emotional tie, so important for childhood. When the Oedipus complex and its intense object relationships towards the parents come to an end, the child has to compensate for this loss of objects. Its identifications with its parents, which have probably been there for some time, become vastly intensified. Similar identifications, the precipitates of abandoned object attachments, recur often enough later on in childhood. But the emotional importance of this first case of such a transformation is suitably marked by the special position given in the ego to its product. Analysis shows that the super-ego is impaired if the Oedipus complex has not been successfully overcome.

In the course of its growth the super-ego is also influenced by those adults who have taken the place of the parents by being concerned with the child's upbringing. In the normal course of events the super-ego edges further and further away from the parents to become in the end impersonal. An additional factor to be remembered is that the child views its parents differently at different periods of its life. At the point where the Oedipus complex makes way for the super-ego the parents are splendid figures in the child's eyes. Later on they lose much of their prestige. The child may identify himself with these later editions of the parents as well. These identifications furnish important contributions to the formation of its character. But they only influence the ego. They have no effect on the super-ego, which has been determined by the child's earliest images of its parents.

Among the important activities ascribed to the super-ego is that of being the vehicle of the ego ideal. The ego ideal sets the standard by which the ego measures itself. It is also the goal towards which it strives and the summons to pursue ever increasing perfection. This ego ideal is no doubt precipitated by the child's early admiration for its supposedly perfect parents.

The So-called "Inferiority Complex"

Consideration of this quest for perfection raises the question of the sense of inferiority which is said to distinguish the neurotic. For some reason or other it has caught the public fancy and found its way into literary productions of every kind. As Freud remarked: "A writer who brings in the phrase 'inferiority complex' thinks he has satisfied all the demands of psycho-analysis and raised his work on to a higher psychological plane." As a matter of fact psycho-analysts hardly ever use the phrase, which does not refer to anything which they regard as elementary or even simple. The school of psychologists who follow Adler attribute this inferiority complex to the perception in oneself of some organic disability. Freud regarded this as a mistake. He insisted that the sense of inferiority has a strong erotic basis. The child who perceives that it is not loved feels inferior. The adult, too, for that matter. The only organ really regarded as inferior is the girl's clitoris. But the sense of inferiority arises for the most part out of the relationship of the ego to the super-ego. Like the sense of guilt it is an expression of the tension between them—and in fact the two are very difficult to distinguish. It may be that the sense of inferiority is the erotic counterpart to the sense of guilt.

On the subject of the inferiority complex in literature Freud was somewhat scornful. Here is what he had to say about one example, easily recognizable as Emil Ludwig's *Life of Kaiser Wilhelm II*: "The author has made an attempt to build up the whole development of his hero's character on the basis of a sense of inferiority, caused by the mal-development of a limb which was injured at birth. While doing this he has overlooked a small but not unimportant fact. It is usual for mothers to whom fate has given a sickly or otherwise defective child to try to compensate for this unfair handicap with an extra amount of love. In this case the proud mother behaved quite differently; she withdrew her love from the child on account of his disability. When the child grew up into a man of great power he proved beyond all doubt by his behaviour that he had never forgiven his mother. If we only bear in mind the importance of mother-love for the mental life of the child we shall be able to make the necessary corrections in the biographer's inferiority theory."

To return to the super-ego. It has been assigned the duties of self-observation, conscience, and the maintenance of ideals. It is based upon two momentous facts which are closely bound up with one another. One is the biological fact that the human child depends on its parents for a very long time. The other is the psychological fact of the Oedipus complex. The super-ego stands for all moral restrictions and for the impulse towards perfection. It is the psychological instrument, so to speak, of what people call the "higher" things in life. We have traced it back to the influence of parents, nurses, teachers, and the other adults who have a hand in its upbringing. The fact that these are its sources teaches us something of its significance. For in bringing up children adults as a rule follow the dictates of their own super-egos. Their ego may be on easy terms with their super-ego, but when it comes to the training of the child they are apt to be exacting. They forget the difficulties of their own childhood and are glad to be able at long last to identify themselves fully with their own parents, whom they remember as putting severe restraints on them. So the super-ego of the child is built on the model not of the parents themselves but of their super-ego. It is thus the vehicle of tradition. Through it are handed down from generation to generation the traditional age-old values. The recognition of the super-ego is a great help in understanding man's social behaviour and such problems as delinquency. It may perhaps provide some useful light for education.

The "Higher" Things in Life

MORALITY [1]

How does an individual attain to a higher plain of morality? One answer that is sometimes given is that he is good and noble from his birth. A more plausible answer is that we are dealing with a process of development. It will probably assume that the development takes the form of eradicating evil tendencies and, by means of education and a civilized environment, replacing them by good ones. This theory is then faced with the problem that evil should still be so powerful in those who have had all the benefits of this education.

But this theory takes it for granted that there is such a thing as the eradication of evil tendencies. Psycho-analytical investigations lends no countenance to this assumption. On the contrary it shows that the foundation of human nature consists of elemental instincts, neither good nor bad in themselves, which are common to all men and aim at the satisfaction of certain primal needs. It is we who label them and their manifestations as good or evil, and we do so according as they meet or do not meet the needs and demands of the community. Admittedly all those instincts which society condemns are of this primitive type, e.g. selfishness and cruelty.

But these primitive instincts are subject to a long process of development before they are allowed to express themselves in the adult. They are inhibited, they get diverted to other aims, they alter their objects, they mingle, and to some extent they are turned back upon their owner. Reaction-formations against certain instincts take a delusive form. The content is changed—egoism into altruism, cruelty into pity. These reaction-formations are all the easier to carry out because many instincts express themselves almost from the outset in pairs of opposites. This remarkable fact is called "ambivalence" of feeling. The most obvious instance is the fact that intense love and intense hatred often exist side by side in the same person. Psycho-analysis adds that the pair of contrary feelings are often directed towards the same person.

Reaction-Formations

In every individual the instincts go through a history that is checkered with vicissitudes. Not till these have been surmounted is the character formed. And, as we all know, characters can

[1] Coll. Pap., vol. iv, pp. 295–303 [Thoughts for the times on war and death].

"Good" and "Bad" Character

only be classified as "good" and "bad" by very simple-minded persons, since a human being is rarely altogether the one or the other. The usual situation is that a person is good in one relation and bad in another. It has often been noticed that the existence of strong "bad" impulses in infancy may be the actual condition for a definite inclination towards "good" in the adult. Childhood egoists may turn into the most helpful and self-sacrificing members of the adult community, while most of our sentimentalists, friends of humanity and champions of animals, have been evolved from little sadists and tormentors of cats and dogs.

Egoistic and Social Instincts

Two factors, an internal and an external, co-operate in transforming our "bad" instincts. The internal factor is the influence exercised by erotism, that is, by the need for love in its widest sense. The admixture of erotic components transforms the egoistic instincts into social ones. Being loved is, we find, worth the sacrifice of certain other advantages. The external factor is the influence of upbringing which presses the claims of our cultural environment and is later on strengthened by the whole force of the civilization surrounding us. Civilization is the fruit of the renunciation of instinctual satisfaction by countless generations. It exacts the same renunciation from each newcomer. Throughout the life of the individual outside compulsion is being constantly replaced by internal compulsion. The pressures of civilization together with the admixture of erotic elements cause an ever-increasing transmutation of egoistic trends into altruistic and social ones. In the last resort every internal compulsion which has served to foster the development of human beings was originally an external one. The child who is born to-day brings with him an inherited disposition towards the transmutation of egoistic into social instincts, and this disposition is easily stimulated into effective action. A further measure of transformation has to be achieved during the individual's own lifetime. In this way the human being is under the pressure not only of his immediate and contemporary environment, but also of the cultural development accomplished by his forefathers.

Civilization

Cultural Adaptability

An individual's capacity for this transformation—his cultural adaptability—is made up of two parts. One is inborn and the other acquired through experience. The relation of the two to each other and to the untransformed portion of the instinctual life is a very variable one.

On the whole we are inclined to overrate the inborn part. We are also inclined to over-estimate the general adaptability to civilization in comparison with the untransformed instincts—in other words, we are inclined to regard human nature as "better" than it actually is. Our judgment is obscured by another factor which falsifies the issue in the favourable direction.

The impulses of one individual are not visible to another. We only deduce another person's impulses from his behaviour, which we trace to motives arising out of his instinctual life. Our conclusions are bound to be in many cases mistaken. An action which is adjudged "good" from the civilized point of view may be due to a noble motive in the one instance and to an ignoble motive in another. Ethical theorists may classify actions as "good" or "bad" according as they are the outcome of good or bad impulses. But society, which is practical in its aims, pays little attention to this distinction and is well satisfied if a man conducts himself according to the precepts of civilization, whatever his motives may be.

The pressure of education and environment may, as we have seen, bring about a further transformation away from egoism and towards altruism. But this is not the necessary or regular effect of the external compulsion. Education and environment offer other benefits besides love and approval. They employ another kind of premium system—the system of rewards and punishments. Their effect may thus be good behaviour without any enoblement of instinct or transformation of inclinations. From the point of view of society it will not make much difference. And only a peculiar set of circumstances will show that *A* always acts rightly from instinctual inclination, while *B* only does so in so far and for as long as it is advantageous for his own egoistic purposes. Since superficial acquaintance will not enable us to distinguish between the two types, we are easily misled into grossly exaggerating the number of people whose instincts have been transformed.

Education

Social Suppression of Instincts

Civilization is thus often only skin deep. A good many people obey the demand for good conduct, but are not thereby following the dictates of their own natures. Encouraged by this success society has gone on to pitch the moral standard higher and higher, so estranging its members still further from their instinctual dispositions. The strain of an unceasing suppression of instincts betrays itself in the most astonishing phenomena of reaction and compensation formations. In the sphere of sexuality, where the suppression is most difficult to enforce, we see the reaction phenomena of neurotic disorders. In other spheres the strain produces no pathological results, but its results are seen in malformations of character and in the perpetual readiness of the inhibited instincts to seize any opportunity to gratify themselves. An individual who is continually obliged to obey precepts which do not tally with his instinctual inclinations is living, psychologically, beyond his means. From a purely objective point of view he might be called a hypocrite. There can be no question that our civilization to-day fosters this form of hypocrisy in a high degree. It might even be said that our civilization is founded on it. If people undertook to live in accordance with their true psychological inclinations our civilization would have to undergo very extensive modifications. There are very many more hypocrites than truly civilized persons. It may be maintained that a certain modicum of civilized hypocrisy is indispensable if civilization is to be upheld, because the cultural adaptability attained by contemporary man seems inadequate to the task. The maintenance of civilization even on so uncertain a basis does at least offer the prospect that each new generation may achieve a further transmutation of instinct and become the pioneer of a higher form of civilization.

Civilized Hypocrisy

Survival of Former Psychological Stages

The evolution of the mind shows a peculiarity which is exhibited in no other process of development. When a village grows into a town or a child grows into a man the village and the child become submerged in the town and the man. The old materials and forms are superseded by new ones and only memory can discover the earlier features in the later product. With the development of the mind we get the peculiar state of affairs that each earlier stage persists alongside the later stage which has developed from it. The successive stages co-exist in spite of the fact that the whole series refers to the same materials. An earlier mental state may have disappeared from view for many years, but it remains in existence and may at any time again become the mode of expression of the forces of the mind. It may even do so to the exclusion of all other modes, as though all the later developments had been annulled. This remarkable plasticity is not unlimited in scope. It might be described as a special capacity for regression, since it may well happen that a later stage of evolution when once abandoned cannot be recovered.

But the primitive stages can always be re-established; the primitive mind is literally imperishable.

To the layman what are called mental diseases give an impression of destruction of the life of mind and soul. In reality it is only the later stages of development that are destroyed. The essence of mental disease is a return to earlier forms of affective life and functions.

Sleep gives an excellent example of the plasticity of mental life. We desire sleep every night. The interpretation of dreams shows that, when we sleep, we cast off our hard-won morality like a garment and only put it on again next morning. We can do this without any risk because sleep puts us in a state of inactivity. In our dreams we can see the regression of our emotional life to its earliest stages of development. It is noteworthy, for example, that all our dreams are governed by purely egoistic motives. Even the most high-minded altruist is a straightforward egoist in his dreams.

The transformation of instinct on which our cultural adaptability is founded may also be undone, temporarily or permanently, by the experiences of life. War is undoubtedly one of the influences that can bring about such regression. Under the circumstances of war individuals will throw off the customary restraints and indulge in uncivilized behaviour. In doing so they at least show some flexibility and we may anticipate that with the return of peace their instincts will be restored to their former level of refinement.

Emotions and Intelligence

Philosophers and students of human nature have long been aware that the intelligence is not an independent force, out of reach of the influence of emotions. They have taught us that, on the contrary, we must rescue it from the influence of strong emotional impulses if it is to function reliably. Left under those influences it is an instrument of the will and obediently produces the conclusions that the will asks for. In their opinion logical arguments are powerless against strong emotional interests. That is why reasons, though "as plenty as blackberries" (in Falstaff's phrase), so seldom triumph in the conflict with interests. The experience of psycho-analysis confirms this view, if further confirmation were necessary. It shows that the most reasonable persons will suddenly behave like imbeciles when their intelligent insight collides with an emotional resistance, but will completely regain their customary acumen as soon as the resistance has been overcome.

A DIFFICULTY IN PSYCHO-ANALYSIS [1]

The theory of psycho-analysis presents a good many difficulties. By " difficulty " we are not thinking of something that makes it hard to understand, but of something that arouses opposition and makes a reader disinclined to believe in it or take an interest in it. That is to say, it is an affective difficulty, not an intellectual one. The two kinds of difficulty may easily amount to the same thing, for where sympathy is lacking, understanding will not come readily.

Psycho-analysis began with the experience of a large number of observations and impressions. Out of these there at last shaped itself something like a theory. It is known as the libido theory. The practical purpose of psycho-analysis is to explain and cure what are called nervous disorders. In tackling this problem a starting-point had to be found somewhere. It was decided to look for it in the life of the instincts. Hypotheses concerning the instincts came therefore to form the basis of the psycho-analytical conception of nervous disease.

Libido Theory

Academic psychology, which gives very unsatisfactory replies to questions regarding our mental life, is in no direction so unsatisfactory as in this matter of the instincts. Psycho-analysis was left to take soundings in its own way.

The popular view distinguishes between hunger and love, seeing in them the representatives of those instincts which aim at self-preservation in the one case and reproduction of the species in the other. This is a very obvious distinction to make. Psycho-analysis also postulates a similar distinction between the self-preservative or ego instincts and the sexual instincts. The force by which the sexual instinct is represented in the mind is given the name of " libido "—sexual hunger. It is analogous to the force of hunger, the will to power, and other similar trends among the ego tendencies.

Starting out from this point psycho-analysis made its first important discovery : that when we try to understand neurotic disorders by far the greatest significance attaches to the sexual instincts. Neuroses are, so to speak, the specific disorders of the sexual function. It is generally true that whether a person develops a neurosis or not depends on the strength of his libido

[1] Coll. Pap., vol. iv, pp. 347–356 [A difficulty of Psycho-Analysis].

and the possibility of gratifying it and thereby discharging it. The form taken by the disorder is determined by the path which the sexual development of the patient has followed—by the fixations his libido has undergone. It was found, further, that by a special and not very simple technique for influencing the mind it is possible to illuminate the nature of many groups of neuroses and at the same time to resolve them. The greatest therapeutic success has been scored with a certain class of neuroses originating in a conflict between ego instincts and sexual instincts. For it may happen that the demands of the sexual instinct, involving as they do other people, seem to the ego to threaten his self-preservation or his self-respect. The ego, as a defensive measure, denies the sexual instincts the gratification they seek and drives them into those by-paths of substitute gratification which then exhibit themselves as symptoms of a neurosis.

The technique of treatment is able to reverse this process of repression and so bring about a better solution of the conflict, a solution compatible with health.

" One-Sidedness of Psycho-analysis "

Psycho-analysts are accused of over-estimating the sexual instincts. Their opponents protest that human beings have other interests besides sex. This is not forgotten or denied. Freud wrote : " Our one-sidedness is like that of the chemist who traces all compounds back to the force of chemical attraction. In doing so he does not deny the force of gravity ; he leaves that to the physicist to reckon with."

Narcissism

In the course of treating a patient the analyst has to consider the distribution of his libido. He looks for the objects, or ideas of them, to which it is attached and then frees it from them so that it shall be at the disposal of the ego. The experience of therapeutic practice has led analysts to a very curious picture of the direction taken by man's libido at the start of life. They have been led to conclude that at the beginning all the erotic tendencies, all capacity for love, is directed towards the self. It is only later that, in association with the satisfaction of the principal natural functions, the libido flows out towards objects beyond the self. Not until this point is reached is it possible to distinguish the libidinal trends from the ego instincts. It is possible for the progress to be undone and for the libido to detach itself from these objects and revert to the original self-love.

The condition in which the libido is contained within the ego was named by Freud *narcissism*, after the youth who remained faithful to his love for his own reflection. The development of the individual is a progress from narcissism to object love. But the libido is never wholly transferred to objects outside the ego. Even when object love is highly developed some degree of narcissism persists. The ego is, in Freud's words, " a great reservoir from which the libido that is destined for objects flows outward and into which it can flow back from those objects." For complete health the libido should not lose this mobility. It is rather like an amœba, which puts out elongations into which the substance of its body extends, but can retract them again at any time so that the original form is reinstated.

The libido theory of the neuroses is the foundation of the psycho-analytical conception of their nature and the psycho-analytical treatment for relieving them. Psycho-analysts regard its premises as valid for normal behaviour too. The term narcissism is employed in relation to little children in the course of their normal development as well as of neurotics. It was excessive narcissism in primitive man that made him think that his own thoughts were omnipotent and that he could therefore influence the course of external events by magical practices.

The Thrice-Wounded Human Narcissism

On a much earlier page we mentioned that the self-love of humanity — the general narcissism of man—has suffered three severe blows from the researches of science. Let us consider them now in a little more detail.

The Cosmological Blow

When men first began to wonder about their dwelling-place, the earth, they came to the conclusion that it was the stationary centre of the Universe, with the sun, moon, and planets circling round it. This was a natural if naïve conclusion from the evidence of their senses. Man felt no movement in the earth. Wherever he had a clear view he found himself the centre of a circle that embraced the whole world outside him. That the world was the centre of the universe showed its sovereignty in the universe, and this fitted in very nicely with his disposition to regard himself as lord of the world.

The destruction of this narcissistic illusion is associated with the name of Copernicus in the sixteenth century. But centuries earlier the Pythagoreans had already cast doubt on the privileged position of the earth, and in the third century B.C.

Aristarchus of Samos had asserted that the earth moved round the sun and was much smaller than it. The great discovery of Copernicus had, therefore, been made before. But when it exacted general recognition the self-love of humanity suffered its first great wound.

The Biological Blow

At a very early stage in his development man acquired a dominating position over his fellow creatures. Encouraged by this supremacy he began to place a great gulf between his nature and theirs. They did not possess reason. He did. He had an immortal soul. He even claimed Divine descent. There could be no common bond between him and the animal kingdom. It is interesting to notice that this piece of arrogance is still as foreign to the small child as it is to the primitive man. It belongs to a later and more pretentious stage. At the level of totemism man sees nothing derogatory in tracing his descent from an animal ancestor. In myths, which contain the deposit of this ancient attitude, the gods take animal shape. In the art of pre-historic times and even of ancient Egypt they are portrayed with animals' heads. The tremendous difference between human nature and the nature of animals is not obvious to a child. He is very ready to accept thinking and talking animals in fairy tales. He bestows on a dog or a horse emotions like those he bestows on human beings—without intending any insult to the human beings. It is only later that he becomes so far estranged from the animals as to use their names for the purposes of abuse.

In the middle of the nineteenth century the researches of Darwin, his collaborators, and predecessors, put an end to this presumption on the part of man. Man is not a being with a separate origin from the animals. His ancestry is in the animal race and is more closely related to some of its members and more distantly to others. Whatever has been added in the course of his later development has not sufficed to remove the evidences of his kinship with them, both in his physical structure and in his mental make-up. This was the second blow to human narcissism.

The Psychological Blow

The third blow is probably the most wounding of all. Man might feel humbled in his relations to the universe and the animal kingdom, but he feels himself supreme in his own soul. Somewhere at the very heart of his ego he has developed a faculty which keeps watch on his impulses and actions to see that they comply with its demands. If they do not they are sternly forbidden. His inner perception, his consciousness, keeps the ego informed of all the main occurrences in the mind's working, and the will, set in motion by these reports, proceeds to carry out what the ego orders and to modify whatever tends to happen independently. This soul of man's is not a simple thing. It is a hierarchy of superior and subordinate agents, a labyrinth of impulses straining towards action independently of one another and corresponding with the multiplicity of instincts and of relations with the external world, many of which are mutually conflicting and incompatible. If there is to be co-ordinated action at all, the highest of these agents must know what is going on and its will must penetrate everywhere to exert its influence. The ego feels quite sure that the reports it receives are reliable and complete and that the channels by which it can enforce its will are equally trustworthy.

In certain disorders, including the neuroses, things are different. The ego has no such feeling of confidence and security, because it finds a limit set to its power in its own house. Thoughts suddenly break in and the conscious mind neither knows where they come from nor can it thrust them away again. They seem more powerful than those which are at the ego's command. They are impervious alike to logical refutation and all the well-tried techniques of the will. Even inconsistence with reality leaves them unshaken. And there are impulses which seem so alien that the ego disowns them. Yet it is afraid of them and takes precautions against them. It feels as though it had been invaded. It increases its vigilance, but to no avail, and it cannot understand why it feels so strangely paralysed.

Once upon a time such things were regarded as intrusion into the mind by evil spirits. Orthodox psychiatry rejects this, of course, but after that it can only say with a shrug: "Degeneracy—hereditary disposition—constitutional inferiority." Psycho-analysis seeks to explain these sinister disorders. That is the purpose of its laborious investigations and its hypotheses. On the strength of its experience, it says (in Freud's words) to the ego: "Nothing has entered into you from without; a part of the activity of your own mind has been withdrawn from your knowledge and from the command of your will. That, too, is why you are so weak in your defences; with one part of your forces you are fighting the other part and you cannot concentrate the whole of your energy as you would against an outer enemy. And it is not even the worst or least effective part of your mental powers that has thus become antagonistic to you and independent of you. The blame lies with yourself. You overestimated your strength when you thought you could do as you liked with your sexual instincts and could utterly ignore their aims. The result is that they have rebelled and have gone their own way in the dark to rid themselves of this oppression; they have extorted their rights in a manner you cannot sanction. How they have achieved this and the paths by which they have reached their purpose, you have not learnt; only the result of their work, the symptom which you experience as suffering, has come to your knowledge. Then you do not recognize it as a product of your own rejected impulses and do not know that it is a substitutive gratification of them."

That this should be possible at all is due to the single fact that the ego is under a very important misapprehension. It believes itself to be informed of everything of any consequence that goes on within the mind, thanks to the news service conducted by consciousness. Under this delusion you confidently assume that nothing can exist in your mind without your knowledge. In other words the mind is regarded as co-extensive with consciousness. People hug this delusion despite the most obvious evidence that a great deal more is constantly going on in your mind than your consciousness is aware of. We now know that what is in our minds and what we are conscious of are not one and the same thing. It is true, fortunately, that in the ordinary way the consciousness is well enough informed to meet our needs. We may harbour the illusion that we at least get wind of all the more important happenings within our minds. But the fact of the matter is that the news we receive is always incomplete and is often quite untrustworthy. It is not only that in such cases as a conflict between instincts the intelligence service breaks down and the will then extends no further than the information we receive. It happens only too often that we do not get news of what has taken place until it is all over and we can no longer do anything to arrest or alter it. We behave like an absolute monarch who contents himself with the information furnished by his highest officials and never goes among the people to find out what they are thinking. Even when we are not ill a great deal is going on in our minds of which we are ignorant or misinformed. What the psycho-analyst says to the patient is in effect: "Look into the depths of your own soul and learn to know yourself. Then you will understand why this illness was bound to come upon you and perhaps you will avoid falling ill in future."

This is the way in which psycho-analysis seeks to educate the ego. But these two discoveries—that the life of the sexual instincts cannot be totally restrained, and that mental processes are in themselves unconscious and only reach the ego and its control through incomplete and unreliable perceptions—amount to saying that the ego is not master in its own house. This is the third great wound inflicted on man's self-love—a psychological one, to follow the cosmological and biological blows. It is not surprising, therefore, that the ego puts up so strong a resistance to the teachings of psycho-analysis.

Few people realize the enormous significance for science and for life of the recognition of unconscious mental processes. Psycho-analysis does not claim to be the discoverer of their existence. It was preceded by a number of philosophers, in particular Schopenhauer, whose unconscious " Will " has many characteristics of the instincts as seen by psycho-analysis. It was Schopenhauer who in words of unforgettable impressiveness admonished man that his sexual craving had a degree of importance which he had not—and still has not—fully appreciated. The achievement of psycho-analysis is that it has gone beyond asserting these two humiliating propositions on an abstract basis—the importance of sexuality in the mind and the unconsciousness of mental activity. It has demonstrated them in matters that affect every individual intimately and compel him, once he has heard of them, to take up some attitude towards these problems. This is what has brought on it the aversion and hostility which general deference or general ignorance spared the philosopher.

POSTSCRIPT: CONCERNING SOME DIFFICULTIES

Let us assume that a sociologist, having read the foregoing pages, sees no reason to doubt the validity of Freud's conclusions. He is prepared to make use of them, as need arises, in his sociological work. Nevertheless he will as a rule want to put a few additional questions first. Frequently the first question is: "How is it possible to reduce the great variety of social behaviour patterns, not merely of our contemporaries, but also of people living at different historical periods, to such an apparently small number of basic psychological mechanisms? Obviously, there are considerable differences of behaviour between persons of different social classes and different historical periods. And yet you wish us to believe that the psychological mechanisms discovered by Freud are capable to a considerable extent of explaining the behaviour of them all?" This is partly a "philosophical" and partly an empirical question. Philosophically we might wonder that such a multiplicity of different behaviour patterns should be traceable to so few psychological mechanisms. But one might equally well wonder that the numerous and varied states of motion of physical objects can be reduced to the small number of Newtonian laws of motion. This is the essence of a law of nature. A law of physics or a law of psychology does not deny the differences between the manifold processes it explains; it shows what they have in common in spite of their variety. As far as psychology is concerned justifiable surprise need not wait till we come to social psychology.

Reason for such surprise might already be found in the realm of individual psychology. One might ask whether persons who have the same instinctive desire necessarily display the same behaviour. Obviously not; a large number of additional circumstances must be taken into consideration. The mechanism e.g. by means of which a person identifies himself with a model may obviously lead to extremely different behaviour patterns; and these will depend on the characteristics of the model, whether honest or criminal, religious or scientific, impulsive or self-controlled, open or reserved, etc., etc. The same "mechanisms of identification" can be used to explain all the various changes of character which ensue.

Moreover the result will depend to a high degree on the

social milieu in which the process takes place. This was convincingly illustrated by Siegfried Bernfeld. Following his line of argument, let us take the case of a little girl who, through identifying herself, say, with an aunt, develops an intensive craving for luxury, which successfully resists every attempt at sublimation. What becomes of the girl will depend very much upon the social milieu in which she finds herself. If her lot is cast in the circumstances of a proletarian existence, with its lack of opportunity to rise in the social scale, her attempt to satisfy her desire for luxury may easily land her in prostitution. If she comes of a middle-class family with its rigid moral code and restricted finances the " way out " that will offer itself will be that of compulsion neurosis ; by her suffering she will punish herself for her desires, while at the same time achieving a substitute satisfaction by staying at a nursing home. In an upper-class family, able to gratify the daughter's desire for luxury, she will grow up as a " spoilt " child, take her fill of amusement as a young girl, and when married will either worthily represent her husband or ruin him financially.

It is clear that the varying " degrees of liberty " in society, with their corresponding restrictions, lead to the development of extremely varied overt behaviour patterns. The psychoanalytical insight into the variety of possible vicissitudes of instinct requires to be supplemented by knowledge of the social conditions, if we are to trace the motives of behaviour in either the individual or the group. Without co-operation between the sociologist and the psychologist the actual behaviour is unpredictable.

Naturally this applies not only to different social milieus within a given society, but even more to the variations of human behaviour in different types of society.

It is obvious, for example, that the desire to get rich calls for a different kind of behaviour in the twentieth century from what it did in the eighteenth century. The son of a twentieth-century industrialist is hardly likely to succeed in business following the rules of conduct which a citizen of the fourteenth century would have recommended to his heir. It is also obvious that similar types of character have unequal chances of success in different historical periods. The by no means easy task of every human being is, with the instinct structure given him by nature and the conditioning effected by society and education, either to adapt himself to the existing order of things or to transform or revolutionize it more or less consciously and directly. All changes in that social order are brought about in the course of history in a very indirect manner; and it is the sociologist rather than the psychologist who must make the main contribution to their explanation. The invention of new machines, the development of new productive forces, and the emergence of novel production relations change the conditions of life of the men and the institutions which they create; these developments lead individuals and groups into new behaviour patterns, which are reproduced by means of education until such time as a fresh development leads to another change in the behaviour patterns.

To what extent this process changes not only the behaviour produced by the psychological mechanisms, but the mechanisms themselves I am unable to say. So far there has hardly been any attempt to develop a discipline of "comparative psychology"—not merely descriptive but explanatory—analogous to "comparative anatomy". Some of the tentative contributions made by psychologists inspire little confidence because of their sociological innocence. It does not, however, appear to me that the behaviour of men in earlier times makes the assumption of divergent instinct endowments or the existence of divergent psychological mechanisms inescapable. In any case the changes in the social conditions under which human behaviour is produced and reproduced in the course of the development of the social productive forces, furnish in the meantime abundant material for the investigation of the causes of the actual variety of psychological behaviour of individuals and groups. We might say with Occam: "Entia non sunt multiplicanda praeter necessitatem"; or, freely translated: "Let us first see how far we can get with pre-analytical and analytical means of explanation."

It would seem to me, though, that "psycho-analytical" explanations sometimes go beyond what is desirable and land one in a wide field of unrealistic considerations which I should like to term "pseudo-social psychology".

For instance the waging of war in human society is explained by the aggressive instinct and it is asserted that warfare, just as much as this instinct, is part and parcel of what people choose to call "human nature". This argument cheerfully overlooks the fact that in human history there occur considerable and lengthy periods of unbroken peace, whilst instincts are admittedly a more or less permanent institution. (Perhaps we are asked to assume that the grandchildren make up for their grandparents' shortcomings in aggressiveness.)

What the psycho-analytical theory of instincts really teaches is that instincts can be deflected far from their primary aims (so far that sadism can be transformed into pity). Thus even if one fell in with the absurd assumption that the waging of war was some sort of primary aim of the destructive instincts, this would point to the *possibility* of wars, but it would not imply that they are actually bound to take place. Seriously, one could hardly go beyond maintaining that the aggressive inclination of human beings is a *necessary* but by no means *sufficient* precondition for the occasional waging of war. Since men ceased living in rival packs wars have been extremely indirect consequences of the social mechanism—foreseen by few and, it may be, intended by even fewer. They are, like the major part of historical transactions, results of social activities whose participants hardly contemplate war and in which the aggressive instinct need not so much as play a decisive part. I can imagine that when a board meeting of an armament concern reaches decisions which ultimately result in a war the directors, when making their fateful decisions, feel far from aggressive either consciously or unconsciously.

To explain many of the acts which human beings perform during a war (and not only then) requires the assumption of strongly destructive inclinations. These inclinations are, however, just as incapable of " explaining " wars as, for instance, variations in " love " are of explaining the rise or fall of the birth-rate. This example may appear rather crude, but it seems to me very much of a piece with those pseudo-social-psychological theories for whose purposes I should not like to see analytical psychology misused. After the pseudo-biological use of Darwin's theories one would like to be spared the experience of the pseudo-psychological use of Freud's theories in sociology.

There are countless problems of war psychology capable of legitimate analytical treatment. But one must not look for them in the sphere of generalities. They vary from one war to another according to the national and social traditions of the belligerents, their social background, their age, their type of character, and their ideological attitudes.

Psycho-analysis has occupied itself in a so to speak " professional " capacity, with a number of questions of war-psychology, such as e.g. the fear of death, panic, war neurosis, psychological consequences of children's evacuation, permanent shelter life, etc. If one were to go further and begin seriously investigating the attitude of various groups towards war and their behaviour during war, in the past as well as in the present, it would be most unwise to use pre-analytical methods for this purpose, for too large a portion of the psychological processes to be explored lies below the surface of consciousness.

How could one, for example, examine the psychology of national feeling during wartime without explaining by analytical methods how men come to transfer to the conceptions of Fatherland and Mother Tongue emotions derived from the personal sphere—as is still apparent from the words they use. The occupation of that land, the suppression of that tongue are felt and revenged as personal insults. The protest is reinforced by infantile ties, which impart to the emotion its special colouring and add to its strength. To anyone who feels thus Goethe's saying does not apply : " The downfall of the fatherland is a phrase, a burning house is reality "—for that downfall releases the same type of emotion that would accompany the burning down of the paternal house.

The education we are given creates that readiness to transfer emotions, which is meant to imbue the citizen with the same respectful and authority-fearing attitude towards the state as he had towards his parents ; as Fromm once said, the family is the ideology-factory of society.

These remarks should not be misunderstood ; what is thus created is the *possibility* of such emotional transferences. Whether they *actually* occur depends on hundreds of further social and psychological factors. Not least on whether an intellectually and morally mature person finds his opinions in agreement with his emotional preparedness ; whether, for instance, during his development " mankind " has taken the place of " nation ", or his " class " that of the " state " ; whether he approves to-day of what he was once taught to love ; whether he is capable of shifting his emotions according to his convictions or whether his convictions are compulsorily swayed by his emotions.

All investigations of this kind involve the danger of rationalizing and also of " irrationalizing "—the danger of either wanting to sever the reality of the present from the emotions of the past or, fascinated by them, of ignoring the impact of reality.

Sociologists ought to be aware of the trap into which this

" rationalization " may lead them, whilst at the same time obligingly warning analysts off the path of " irrationalization ". " Rationalized " and " irrationalized " social-psychological descriptions and explanations are equally tiresome.

I might equally well have cited the psychology of group-formation or ideology-formation as a warning example of ignorance or misuse of analytical concepts and theories.

Freud himself made the most important analytical contribution towards the psychology of group-formation in his book *Group Psychology and the Analysis of the Ego*. As the analytical psychology of the individual had already in its mode of approach realized the full importance of the family group (since psycho-analytical theory knows no Robinson Crusoes whose entire behaviour is spun out of their own " nature "), it is only natural that in the behaviour of the group it saw reflected all the features it had observed in the individual : it found the attitude to the leader reflecting the attitude to the father, in its positive as well as in its negative aspects, the attitude towards comrades in arms reflecting that towards brothers and sisters, the ideology promulgated by the leader corresponding to the father's moral concepts. The increase in understanding of what takes place emotionally within a group was considerable. The readiness to submit or to revolt lost its mysteriousness. The heightening of the group member's courage and, alternatively, his state of complete helplessness if the group falls apart were no longer a riddle. Through the understanding of these mechanisms the " group soul " had been exorcized from mass psychology in the same way as the individual " soul " had been eliminated by the theory of the psychological mechanisms from individual psychology.

Social psychology only comes to grief when one supposes that merely with the knowledge of those mechanisms that operate in groups one can understand or infer the actual behaviour of groups in the course of history, when every conservative is regarded as a " protagonist of the father idea ", and every revolutionary as a prospective father-image murderer, when every quarrel and every split inside a group are treated as just another version of strife between brothers, and every victory and defeat interpreted in terms of the internal cohesion of the group members.

It is only in rare cases that Freud's mass psychology is so grossly misunderstood. It seems to me, however, that the more subtle misuses of it are also caused in the same way : the emotional possibilities of the group member are not simply used as part explanation of his actual behaviour, but the necessity of his actual behaviour is supposedly inferred from them.

Thus it is not that the passion for collecting of the " anal " type of character is considered to contribute towards a banker's success ; the origin of banking is " explained " by the existence of a majority of " anal types of character " during a certain historical period. (It is true that a stable society produces something like the types of character it needs. But as it continually changes its structure owing to the laws of economic development the individual is not spared the necessity of further adaptation or opposition.)

Analytical group *psychology*—which is primarily a psychology of the emotional process—is a subdiscipline of that branch of sociology whose subject is the social behaviour of groups. It is capable of interpreting the group-individual's emotional possibilities of behaviour ; but how the groups and their individual members actually behave, can only be explained and predicted when all the historical data relating to the internal and external conditions of the event are available.

The contribution which psycho-analysis has to make to the investigation of ideologies has been the cause of special misunderstandings. The concept of " rationalization ", formulated by Ernest Jones and accepted by Freud, appeared to furnish the psychological counterpart of the sociological concept of " ideology ". Both concepts seemed to place opinions or systems of opinion under a special light. In this light it seemed that opinions depend for their validity on the standpoint of the persons concerned—a standpoint defined in the case of ideology, sociologically, and in the case of " rationalization ", psychologically. To describe a thought in the mind of an individual as a rationalization was regarded as an " exposure " in much the same way as to describe the thought system of a group as " ideological " had formerly been regarded as an " exposure ", unflattering to the thought itself ; and so it was supposed that in the rationalization process the mechanism had been identified which leads to ideology formation. Once again two types of objection—" philosophical " and empirical—were raised against the concept of " rationalization ". The " philosophical " objections were of an epistemological nature and were directed against the " relativism " which was alleged to follow from the concept of rationalization, as from that of ideology.

" How," it is asked, " can we prove the truth of the opinion of an analyst who claims to expose the arguments of another person as a rationalization? What guarantee have we that this exposure is not, in its turn, an equally questionable rationalization on the part of the analyst, intended to refute the other man's arguments by means of an arbitrary interpretation?"

As a consequence of these and similar considerations the critics of analysis often reject the concept of rationalization as leading to an "infinite regress"; or else they accept it, but maintain that its acceptance entails a general "relativity" in the claims to truth of all arguments, and that analysis has to take this into account.

I believe that this epistemological criticism involves an error in logic. When, for instance, an analyst says that someone's line of thought is a rationalization, he is not thereby expressing any opinion as to its rightness or wrongness or as to the correctness of the logical process involved. He is only identifying a particular mechanism of thought. This mechanism is characterized by a discrepancy between what the patient puts forward as the reasons for his opinions and what the analyst can recognize as the motives and causes of those opinions. That the reasons with which one tries to prove an argument, and the motive which causes one to take up that line of argument, can be different, was better known to everyday psychology than to the pre-analytical academic psychology of thought. The German expression "Beweggrund" (actuating reason) for "motive" expresses the error clearly: it seemed a matter of course to the psychologists that it was a man's reasons which actuated his behaviour. Analytical psychology has familiarized us with the fact that many of the reasons which people give for their thoughts and actions are only pretexts which are put forward when the really operative motive is prevented from becoming conscious. The gaps left in our line of argument by the omission of the reason which cannot become conscious are filled by "rationalization", by the rationalized argument. These rationalized arguments are often hastily improvised. One can see this from the fact that they are frequently inadequate, or wrong, or even senseless. And when one considers how they have come into being this is quite understandable. But it is not inherent in the concept of rationalization, which merely signifies a mechanism of thought, and is not concerned with the value of the results. At times it is possible to rationalize correctly, that is, to put forward in place of the motivating argument another one which is capable of becoming conscious and which is at the same time adequate. The business of psycho-analysis is not so much to assess the correctness of a line of thought as to analyse the mechanism which has given rise to it.

In short, the conception of rationalization belongs to the psychology of thought and not to logic. And the subject-matter of the psychology of thought is, to put it roughly, to discover the causal laws which determine the formation of conscious and unconscious trains of ideas which are expressed as " thoughts ", and to explain those " thoughts " as symptoms of the total mental context. To weigh their value as symbols in the apparatus of our language—to judge them from the point of view of logic—is no task of the psychology of thought or of psychology at all. One could, after all, consider a line of argument from the point of view of truth and correct reasoning even if it had been printed in letters which had fallen in the right order from the sky and nobody knew if a " mind " had been at work in its production or not. In such a case there would be nothing for the psychologist of thought to do, whereas the logician could proceed to pass judgment upon it.

If, therefore, one keeps those aspects of the problem which are concerned with the psychology of thought apart from those which are concerned with logic, the epistemological criticisms fall to the ground. In so far as the analyst analyses arguments he reserves his opinion as to their correctness or incorrectness; if and in so far as he undertakes to judge their correctness or incorrectness he uses the criteria of truth which are usual in all sciences. Whether the patient, in the course of his rationalizations about people and things, has made right or wrong judgments, analyst and patient can only decide by turning to the sciences upon whose subject-matter the patient has passed an opinion. It is only when the patient brings rationalized arguments to bear on questions of psychological fact that he finds both the psychologist of thought and the expert on the subject he is arguing about united in the person of the analyst who sits behind him. (I should like to add that I can hardly imagine how a man can possess that quality of self-critical integrity which is, I think, what every scientist demands of himself as a matter of professional ethics unless he is able readily to see through his own rationalizations.)

It is not my task here to prove the soundness of the concept of ideology, but I should be inclined to use analogous arguments.

That opinions are determined by social standpoint does not of itself prove their validity or otherwise. I should think that when a system of thought is being considered as an "ideology", what is meant is that the *social* causes leading to the production and consumption of that system of thought are under examination. One can readily understand that a selection has usually been made from among the various systems of thought, and that attention has been concentrated on the production and consumption of incorrect thoughts. Further the attempt has been made—and I think successfully—to discover under what particular social circumstances the production of either correct or incorrect thoughts is to be expected. The concentration upon wrong ideologies, and wrong rationalization, however, does not alter the fact that it is the causal mechanisms of thought production which are being examined, and that it is impossible in the same operation to decide their correctness. That a thought is proved to have been rationalized does not mean that it has thereby also been discredited.

Now, as examination shows, by no means every incorrect theory whose production has been elucidated along the lines of the sociology of science is a result of a rationalization-mechanism in the heads of the individuals producing it. Besides socially conditioned rationalization there are also socially conditioned shortsightedness (and perspicacity), socially conditioned stupidity (and intelligence), socially conditioned narrow-mindedness (and open-mindedness)—in short all the various shortcomings which hamper the proper understanding of reality.

Conversely an emotion sometimes sharpens our critical discernment. Bitterness about one's own distress may enable one to realize more clearly a particular evil of the social order. The shifting of judgment from personal suffering to social misery may have taken place in the mind of a critic of the social order by means of a rationalization mechanism : in spite of that, or even perhaps for that very reason, the criticism may hit the nail on the head.

As Freud taught his pupils : to use psycho-analytical arguments for polemical (and non-psychological) purposes is inadvisable. This applies, I submit, to the concept of rationalization.

I have now reached the end of my task. First I endeavoured to define the field of co-operation between psycho-analysis and sociology, and to give some idea of the formidable array of problems waiting to be solved. The rendering of Freud's doctrine which followed was designed to provide a survey of the parts of analytical theory essential to the sociologist. I carefully avoided using passages in which Freud himself applied psycho-analytical theories to sociological questions, and confined myself to his psychological theories proper. Thus I made no use of such works as *Totem and Taboo*, *Civilization and its Discontents*, *The Future of an Illusion*, or *Moses*. These works belong to " applied " psycho-analysis. My concern was to set out Freud's views on the foundations of the analytical psychology of the individual—in other words, the psychological contribution which Freud made to social psychology. He himself emphasized more than once that he drew a distinction between his psychological works and his contributions to cultural psychology, and that the latter were highly speculative and controversial in quite a different manner from the real " clinical " discipline of psycho-analysis. I find myself in agreement. Freud had, perhaps without being fully aware of it, based his social-psychological speculations on a quite distinct and particular conception of human society and history, the acceptance or rejection of which is, in my opinion, largely independent of the acceptance of his psychological teachings. Obviously his descriptions of, for instance, the family situation or of contemporary sexual morality imply certain sociological preconceptions. On the other hand I believe that these descriptions can be accepted even from quite a different sociological point of view if some obvious dialectical corrections are made. Our purpose has been to give the sociologist Freud's views not on sociology but on psychology, where he speaks as a master in his own sphere.

Finally I tried to show how, in my opinion, psycho-analysis should *not* be applied to social psychology, if one is not to offend against the spirit of both sociology and psycho-analysis.

Thus this little book will fulfil its purpose if social psychologists use it to make a first acquaintance with analytical theory—in other words (if the presumption may be forgiven) as a kind of first draft for a " Prolegomena to a future social psychology which can claim to rank as a science ".

BIBLIOGRAPHICAL GUIDE

(1) FREUD: LIST OF TRANSLATIONS

(From 1893–1938)[1]

List of Abbreviations

Coll. Pap.—Collected Papers of Sigm. Freud, 4 vols., published by the Institute of Psycho-Analysis (London) and the Hogarth Press.

Int. Psa. Lib.—International Psycho-Analytic Library. Published by the Institute of Psycho-Analysis (London) and the Hogarth Press.

Int. J. Psa.—International Journal of Psycho-Analysis. Published by the Institute of Psycho-Analysis (London) and Bailliere, Tindall, and Cox, Ltd., 8 Henrietta Street, W.C. 1.

Sel. Pap. on Hyst.—Selected Papers on Hysteria. Published in Mental and Nervous Disease Monograph Series (vol. iv), Washington, D.C.

Title of Paper in English.	*Where Published in Translation.*
On the psychical mechanism of hysterical phenomena (in collaboration with Josef Breuer).	Coll. Pap. I and Sel. Pap. on Hyst.
Some points in a comparative study of organic and hysterical paralysis.	Coll. Pap. I
Charcot	Coll. Pap. I
The defence neuro-psychoses	Coll. Pap. I and Sel. Pap. on Hyst.
The case of Miss Lucy R.	Sel. Pap. on Hyst.
The case of Miss Elizabeth v. R. . . .	Sel. Pap. on Hyst.
The Psychotherapy of Hysteria	Sel. Pap. on Hyst.
The justification for detaching from neurasthenia a particular syndrome: the anxiety neurosis.	Coll. Pap. I and Sel. Pap. on Hyst.
A reply to criticisms on the Anxiety Neurosis .	Coll. Pap. I
Obsessions and Phobias: their psychical mechanism and their ætiology.	Coll. Pap. I
Further remarks on the defence neuro-psychoses	Coll. Pap. I and Sel. Pap. on Hyst.
Heredity and the Aetiology of the Neuroses .	Coll. Pap. I
The Aetiology of Hysteria	Coll. Pap. I
Sexuality in the Aetiology of the Neuroses .	Coll. Pap. I

[1] I have to thank Dr. John Rickman for allowing me to use his bibliography, published in the Psycho-Analytical Epitomes, The Hogarth Press, and the Institute of Psycho-Analysis, London.

Title of Paper in English.	*Where Published in Translation.*
The Interpretation of Dreams (London, Allen and Unwin, 1913). [Editions of the translation bearing date from 1933 onwards are to be preferred as at this date the 8th German edition was retranslated.]	
On Dreams (London, Heinemann, 1914) .	Coll. Pap. I
Freud's Psycho-Analytical Method . .	Coll. Pap. I
The Psycho-pathology of Everyday Life (London, Fisher Unwin, 1914).	
On Psychotherapy	Coll. Pap. I and Sel. Pap. on Hyst.
Three Contributions to the Theory of Sexuality (New York, 1910).	
Wit and its Relation to the Unconscious (London, Fisher Unwin, 1916).	
Fragment of an analysis of a case of hysteria .	Coll. Pap. III
My Views on the Rôle of Sexuality in the Aetiology of the Neuroses.	Coll. Pap. I and Sel. Pap. on Hyst.
Psycho-Analysis and the Ascertaining of Truth in Courts of Law.	Coll. Pap. II
Delusion and Dreams (N.Y., Moffat Yard, 1917; London, Allen and Unwin, 1921).	
Obsessive Acts and Religious Practices . .	Coll. Pap. II
The Sexual Enlightenment of Children . .	Coll. Pap. II
"Civilized" Sexual Morality and Modern Nervousness.	Coll. Pap. II
On the Sexual Theories of Children . .	Coll. Pap. II
Hysterical Phantasies and their Relation to Bisexuality.	Coll. Pap. II and Sel. Pap. on Hyst.
Character and Anal Erotism	Coll. Pap. II
The Relation of the Poet to Day-Dreaming .	Coll. Pap. IV
General Remarks on Hysterical Attacks .	Coll. Pap. II
Analysis of a Phobia in a Five-year-old Boy .	Coll. Pap. III
Notes upon a Case of Obsessional Neurosis .	Coll. Pap. III
The Origin and Development of Psycho-Analysis [frequently referred to as "On Psycho-Analysis: Five Lectures" or "The Five Lectures"] (Am. J. Psych., 1910).	
Leonardo da Vinci: A psycho-sexual study of an Infantile Reminiscence (N.Y., 1916; London, Kegan Paul, 1922).	
The Antithetical Sense of Primal Words .	Coll. Pap. IV
The future prospects of Psycho-Analytical Therapy.	Coll. Pap. II and Sel. Pap. on Hyst.
Observation on "wild" Psycho-Analysis .	Coll. Pap. II and Sel. Pap. on Hyst.
Psychogenic Visual Disturbances according to Psycho-Analytical Conceptions.	Coll. Pap. II

Title of Paper in English.	*Where Published in Translation.*
Contributions to the Psychology of Love; A Special Type of Choice of Object Made by Men.	Coll. Pap. IV
Psycho-Analytical Notes upon an auto-biographical account of a case of Paranoia (dementia paranoides).	Coll. Pap. III
Formulations regarding the Two Principles in Mental Functioning.	Coll. Pap. IV
Types of Neurotic Nosogenesis . . .	Coll. Pap. II
Contributions to the Psychology of Love: the most prevalent form of Degradation in Erotic Life.	Coll. Pap. IV
The employment of Dream-Interpretation in Psycho-Analysis.	Coll. Pap. II
The Dynamics of the Transference . .	Coll. Pap. II
Recommendations for Physicians on the Psycho-Analytical Method.	Coll. Pap. II
A Note on the Unconscious in Psycho-Analysis. [Written (in English) at the request of the Society for Psychical Research and first published in a special Medical Supplement of their Proceedings, part lxvi, vol. xxvi.]	Coll. Pap. IV
Further Recommendations in the Technique of Psycho-Analysis: on beginning the treatment, the question of the first communications, the dynamics of the cure.	Coll. Pap. II
A Dream which bore Testimony . . .	Coll. Pap. II
The occurrence in dreams of material from fairy-tales Totem and Taboo (N.Y., Moffat Yard, 1918). On Similarities in the Mental Life of Savages and Neurotics: I. The Dread of Incest. II. Taboo and the Ambivalence of Emotions. III. Animism Magic and the Omnipotence of Thought. IV. The Infantile Return of Totemism.	
The Predisposition to Obsessional Neurosis .	Coll. Pap. II
Infantile Mental Life: Two lies told by Children.	Coll. Pap. II
Fausse Reconnaissance (" deja raconte ") in psycho-analytic treatment.	Coll. Pap. II
The Theme of the Three Caskets . . .	Coll. Pap. IV
On Narcissism: an Introduction . . .	Coll. Pap. IV
The History of the Psycho-Analytic Movement	Coll. Pap. I
The Moses of Michelangelo	Coll. Pap. IV
Further Recommendations in the Technique of Psycho-Analysis: Recollection, Reception, and Working Through.	Coll. Pap. II

Title of Paper in English.	*Where Published in Translation.*
Further Recommendations in the Technique of Psycho-Analysis: Observations on Transference-love.	Coll. Pap. II
A case of Paranoia running counter to the psycho-analytical theory of the disease.	Coll. Pap. II
Thoughts for the times on War and Death (N.Y., Brill and Kuttner, 1918, and Moffat Yard).	Coll. Pap. IV
Instincts and their Vicissitudes . . .	Coll. Pap. IV
Repression	Coll. Pap. IV
The Unconscious	Coll. Pap. IV
Some Character-types met with in psycho-analytic work.	Coll. Pap. IV
A Connection between a Symbol and a Symptom.	Coll. Pap. II
A Mythological Parallel to a Visual Obsession	Coll. Pap. IV
On the Transformation of Instincts with special reference to anal erotism.	Coll. Pap. II
Metapsychological Supplement to the Theory of Dreams.	Coll. Pap. IV
One of the Difficulties of Psycho-Analysis .	Coll. Pap. IV and Int. J. Psa. I
A Childhood Recollection from Dichtung und Wahrheit.	Coll. Pap. IV
Mourning and Melancholia.	Coll. Pap. IV
Introductory Lectures on Psycho-Analysis [delivered 1915–16]. (N.Y., 1920; London, Allen and Unwin, 1922.)	
From the History of an Infantile Neurosis .	Coll. Pap. III
Contributions to the Psychology of Love: The Taboo of Virginity.	Coll. Pap. IV
Turnings in the ways of psycho-analytic therapy	Coll. Pap. II
"A child is being beaten." A contribution to the study of the origin of sexual perversions.	Coll. Pap. II and Int. J. Psa. I
The Uncanny	Coll. Pap. IV
The Psychogenesis of a case of Homosexuality in a Woman.	Coll. Pap. II and Int. J. Psa. I
Beyond the Pleasure Principle . . .	Int. Psa. Lib. 4
Dreams and Telepathy	Coll. Pap. IV and Int. J. Psa. III
Certain Neurotic Mechanisms in Jealousy, Paranoia and Homosexuality.	Coll. Pap. II and Int. J. Psa. IV
Postscript to the Analysis of Little Hans [the 5-year-old boy case, see 1909].	Coll. Pap. III
The Infantile Genital Organization of the Libido: A Supplement to the Theory of Sexuality.	Coll. Pap. II and Int. J. Psa. V

Title of Paper in English.	*Where Published in Translation.*
A Neurosis of Demoniacal Possession in the Seventeenth Century.	Coll. Pap. IV
The Ego and the Id	Int. Psa. Lib. 12
Neurosis and Psychosis	Coll. Pap. II
The Economic Problem in Masochism . .	Coll. Pap. II
The Passing of the Oedipus Complex . .	Coll. Pap. V and Int. J. Psa. V
The Loss of Reality in Neurosis and Psychosis	Coll. Pap. II
Psycho-Analytic Exploring [written in English]. (In " These Eventful Years ". London and N.Y., Enc. Brit. Co., 1924.)	
An Autobiographical Study. [A translation of " Eine Autobiographie Sigmund Freuds " and of " Die Frage der Laienanalyse " bound in one volume was published by Brentano, N.Y., in 1927, under the title of " The Problem of Lay Analyses ".]	Int. Psa. Lib. 26
Negation	Int. J. Psa. VI
Some Psychological Consequences of the Anatomical Distinction between the Sexes.	Int. J. Psa. VIII
Psychoanalysis (London, Enc. Brit., 13th edition).	
Remarks on the Question of Lay Analysis .	Int. J. Psa. VIII
The Problem of Lay Analyses	
Inhibitions, Symptoms, and Anxiety . .	Int. Psa. Lib. 28
Fetishism	Int. J. Psa. IX
The Future of an Illusion	Int. Psa. Lib. 15
Humour	Int. J. Psa. IX
A Religious Experience	Int. J. Psa. X
Civilization and its Discontents . . .	Int. Psa. Lib. 17
Libidinal Types	Int. J. Psa. XIII
Female Sexuality	Int. J. Psa. XIII
The Acquisition of Power over Fire . .	Int. J. Psa. XIII
New Introductory Lectures on Psycho-Analysis	Int. Psa. Lib. 24
Why War? An International Series of Open Letters, No. 2 [with Albert Einstein]. (Paris, Int. Inst. of Intellectual Co-operation.)	
Analysis Terminable and Interminable . .	Int. J. Psa. XVIII
Constructions in Analysis	Int. J. Psa. XIX
Moses—an Egyptian	Int. J. Psa. XX
If Moses was an Egyptian	Int. J. Psa. XX
Moses and Monotheism, 1939, Hogarth Press and The Institute of Psychoanalysis .	
A note on the Wunderblock	Int. J. Psa. XXI
An outline of Psychoanalysis	Int. J. Psa. XXI
Splitting of the Ego in the Defensive Process .	Int. J. Psa. XXII
Medusa's Head	Int. J. Psa. XXII
A disturbance of memory of the Acropolis .	Int. J. Psa. XXII

Title of Paper in English.	*Where Published in Translation.*
Two Encyclopædia Articles: A. Psycho-analysis; B. The Libido Theory.	Int. J. Psa. XXII
Remarks on the Theory and Practice of Dream Interpretation.	Int. J. Psa. XXIII
Some additional notes upon Dream Interpretation as a whole.	Int. J. Psa. XXIII
On Transience	Int. J. Psa. XXIII
My contact with Josef Popper Lynkeus . .	Int. J. Psa. XXIII

The German twelve-volume edition of Freud's Collected Papers, published by the Internationaler Psychoanalytischer Verlag, Vienna, is unfortunately no longer available. The entire stock was destroyed when Austria was invaded by Hitler. A new and complete German edition of Freud's psycho-analytical works in chronological order is in process of publication by the Imago Publishing Co., Ltd., London. It will comprise eighteen volumes, of which several have already appeared. The Index of this edition has been prepared by the author of the present volume, and the headings referring to various subjects might be used as a guide to further study.

(2) BIBLIOGRAPHY ON PSYCHO-ANALYSIS AND SOCIOLOGY

The following section in the bibliography cannot claim to be complete. It consists of papers and books on sociological subjects treated from a (not always orthodox) psycho-analytical point of view. To these items were added a few studies which survey some current discussion between Sociologists and Social Psychologists in a wider sense. Owing to war-time conditions many of the contributions were not available and it is likely that the American literature is not quite adequately represented. Those who aim at completeness will have to consult the psycho-analytical literature, quoted regularly in the pages of the Psychological Abstracts, published by the American Psychological Association, Prince and Lemon Streets, Lancaster, Pa. Perhaps it is unnecessary to state that the inclusion of a book or paper in this bibliography does not imply that the author of that book or paper shares my views of the relation between psycho-analysis and sociology.

LIST OF ABBREVIATIONS

Alm.	Almanach (vol. 1926–1938). Internationaler Psychoanalytischer Verlag, Wien.
Psa. Bew.	Die Psychoanalytische Bewegung. Internationaler Psychoanalytischer Verlag, Wien.
Im.	Imago. Internationaler Psychoanalytischer Verlag, Wien.
Int. J. Psa.	The International Journal of Psycho-Analysis. Baillière, Tindall and Cox, London.
Zeit. f. psa. Päd.	Zeitschrift fuer Psychoanalytische Paedagogik. Verlag der Zeitschrift fuer psychoanalytische Paedagogik, Wien.
Psa. Quart.	The Psychoanalytic Quarterly. The Psychoanalytic Quarterly Inc., 372–4 Broadway, Albany, New York.
Psa. Rev.	The Psychoanalytic Review. New York, 64 West-56th Street.
Rev. Fr. de Psa.	Revue Française de Psychoanalyse, G. Doin et Cte, Editeurs a Paris.
Int. Zeit. f. Psa.	Internationale Zeitschrift fuer Psychoanalyse. Internationaler Psychoanalytischer Verlag, Wien.

I, II, III, etc. . . . No. of volume.

ABRAHAM, K. Dreams and Myths: A Study in Race Psychology. New York, The Journal of Nervous and Mental Disease Publishing Company, 1913.

AICHHORN, A. Kann der Jugendliche straffaellig werden? *Zeit. f. psa. Päd. VIII.* Wayward Youth. New York, Vicking Press, 1935. London, Putnam, 1936.

ALEXANDER, F. The Psychological and Biological Orientations of Psychoanalysis. Mental Hygiene, vol. 1936.
—— Psychoanalysis and Social Disorganization. The American Journal of Sociology, vol. xlii.
—— Our Age of Unreason: A Study of the Irrational Forces in Social Life. Philadelphia, New York, J. B. Lippincott Co., 1942.
—— Educative Influence of Personality Factors in the Environment. Paper read at the Symposium on Environment and Education, University of Chicago, 22nd September, 1941.
—— and STAUB, H. Der Kampf ums Recht. *Psa. Bew. I.*
—— The Criminal, the Judge, and the Public. New York, The Macmillan Company, 1931.
ANDREAS-SALOME, L. Was daraus folgt, dass es nicht die Frau gewesen ist, die den Vater totgeschlagen hat. *Alm. 1928.*
BARTLETT, F. H. Sigmund Freud: A Marxian Essay. London, Victor Gollancz, Ltd., 1938.
BATESON, G. Cultural Determinants of Personality. In J. McV. Hunt ed. Personality and the Behaviour Disorders. New York, 1944.
—— and MEAD, M. Balinese Character. New York, 1942.
BEHRENDT, R. Politischer Aktivismus. Leipzig, 1932. Das Problem Fuehrer und Masse und die Psychoanalyse. *Psa. Bew. I.*
—— Bericht Ueber die Fortschritte der Psychoanalyse in den Jahren, 1914–19. Leipzig, Wien, Zurich, Internationaler Psychoanalytischer Verlag, G.M.B.H.
BERNFELD, S. Der soziale Ort. *Im. XV.*
—— Die Tantalssituation. *Im. XVIII.*
—— "Neuer Geist" contra "Nihilismus". Die Psychologie und ihr Publikum. *Psa. Bew. II.*
—— Sisyphos Oder die Grenzen der Erziehung. Wien, Internationaler Psychoanalytischer Verlag, 1925.
BETTELHEIM, B. Individual and Mass Behaviour in Extreme Situations. Journal of Abnormal and Social Psychology, vol. 38, pp. 417–452 (1943).
BILLINGS, R. A. The Negro and his Church. *Psa. Rev. XXI.*
BONAPARTE, M. Das magische Denken bei Primitiven. *Alm. 1935.*
—— Psychoanalyse und Ethnographie. Das Psychoanalytische Volksbuch, p. 567. Bern, Verlag Hans Huber, 1939.
—— The Myth of the Corpse in the Car. The American Imago, vol. 2, No. 2, pp. 105–126 (1941).
BOOLBY, J. *See* Durbin, E. F. M.
BROWN, J. F. Psychology and the Social Order. New York, 1936.
—— The Origins of the Antisemitic Attitude. In: I. Graeser and S. H. Britt, Jews in a Gentile World. New York, 1942.
BROWN, J. F. The Theory of the Aggressive Urges and War-Time Behaviour. Journal of Social Psychology, vol. 15, pp. 355–380 (1942).
BURGESS, E. W. What Social Case Records should contain to be useful for Sociological Interpretation. Social Forces, vol. 1928.

BURGESS, E. W. Freud and Sociology in the United States. *Am. J. of Soc.*, vol. 45, 1939.
BURLINGHAM, D. *See* Freud, Anna.
BURROW, T. The Social Basis of Consciousness. London, 1927.
BUXBAUM, E. Massenpsychologische Probleme in der Schulklasse. *Zeit. f. psa. Päd. X.*
—— Transference and Group Formation in Children and Adolescents. The Psychoanalytic Study of the Child, vol. i. New York, 1945.
CASEY, R. P. The Psychoanalytic Study of Religion. Journal Abnormal Soc. Psychology, vol. 33, pp. 437–452 (1938).
CHARLES, C. V. Optimism and Frustration in the American Negro. *Psa. Rev. XXIX.*
CHRISTOFFEL, H. Abweichende Richtungen und Schulen. Das Psychoanalytische Volksbuch, p. 667. Bern, Verlag Hans Huber, 1939.
DAI, B. Divided Loyalty in War. Psychiatry, vol. 7, pp. 327–340 (1944).
DALY, C. D. The Psychology of Revolutionary Tendencies. *Int. J. Psa. XI.*
DEVEREUX, G. Social Structure and the Economy of Affective Bonds. *Psa. Rev. XXIX.*
DOLLARD, J. *et al.* Frustration and Aggression. International Library of Sociology and Social Reconstruction. London, Kegan Paul, 1943.
DOLLARD, J. Culture, Society, Impulse, and Socializationum. Am. Journ. of Soc., vol. 45, 1939, pp. 50–63.
—— Caste and Class in a Southern Town. New Haven, 1937.
—— and MILLER. Social Learning and Imitation. New Haven, 1941, and International Library of Sociology and Social Reconstruction. London, Kegan Paul, 1945.
DU BOIS, C. Some Anthropological Perspectives on Psychoanalysis, 24, 246–273.
—— The People of Alor. Minneapolis, 1944.
DURBIN, E. F. M., and BOWLBY, J. Aggressiveness and War. London, Kegan Paul, 1939.
EDER, M. D. (with others). Social Aspects of Psychoanalysis. London, Williams and Norgate, 1924.
EPSTEIN, J. Jesuitismus and Psychoanalyse. *Psa. Bew. II.*
ERICSON, E. Childhood and Tradition in Two American Indian Tribes. In: The Psychoanalytic Study of the Child, vol. i. New York, 1945.
—— Hitler's Imagery and German Youth. Psychiatry, vol. 55, pp. 475–493 (1942).
—— Observation on Sioux Education. J. Psychol., 7, 1939.
FEDERN, P. Maerchen-Mythes-Urgeschichte. Das Psychoanalytische Volksbuch, p. 636. Bern, Verlag Hans Huber, 1939.
FENICHEL, O. Psychoanalysis of Antisemitism. American Imago, 1940, vol. i, pp. 24–39.

FENICHEL, O. The Means of Education. In the Psychoanalytic Study of the Child, 1945 vol.

—— Psychoanalytic Remarks on Fromm's book *Escape from Freedom*. *Psa. Rev.*, vol. 31, pp. 133–152 (1944).

—— Die offene Arbeitskolonie Bolshewo. *Int. J. Psa. XVII.*

—— Psychoanalyse der Politik. *Psa. Bew. IV.*

—— The Clinical Aspect of the Need for Punishment. *Int. J. Psa. IX.*

—— The Drive to Amass Wealth. *Psa. Quart. VII.*

—— The Psychoanalytic Theory of Neurosis. New York, W. N. Norton and Co., 1936 (with very good bibliography).

FERENCZY, S. Bausteine zur Psychoanalyse. Wien, Internationaler Psychoanalytischer Verlag, vol. i, p. 109 ; vol. iii, p. 399.

FLUGEL, J. C. (with others). Social Aspects of Psychoanalysis. London, Williams and Norgate, 1924.

—— The Psychoanalitic Study of the Family. London, The International Psychoanalytical Library, The International Press.

—— The Psychology of Clothes. London, The International Psychoanalytical Library, The Hogarth Press, and the Institute of Psychoanalysis, 1930.

—— Man, Morals, and Society, 1945.

FORSYTH, D. Psychology and Religion. London, Watts and Co., 1935.

FRANK, LAWRENCE K. Freud's Influence on Western Thinking and Culture. The American Journal of Orthopsychiatry, vol. 1940.

FRENCH, T. The Psychodynamic Problem of Democracy. In: G. Watson ed., Civilian Morale. Boston, 1942.

FREUD, A. The Ego and the Mechanisms of Defence. London, The Hogarth Press and the Institute of Psychoanalysis, 1937.

—— (with BURLINGHAM, D.). Infants without Families. London, Geoge Allen and Unwin, Ltd., 1944.

—— —— Young Children in Wartime. London, George Allen and Unwin, Ltd., 1943.

FRENCH, TH. M. Social Conflict and Psychic Conflict. American Journal of Sociol., vol. 1939.

FRIEDLANDER, K. Formation of the Anti-Social Character. The Psychoanalytic Study of the Child, vol. i, 1945.

FROMM, E. Der Staat als Erzieher. *Alm. 1931*, p. iv.

—— Politik und Psychoanalyse. *Psa. Bew. III.*

—— Ueber Methoden und Aufgaben einer analytischen Sozialpsychologie. Zeitschrift fuer Sozialforschung, vol. 1932.

—— Die Entwicklung des Christusdogmas. *Im. XVI.*

—— Sozialpsychologischer Teil in Studien ueber Autoritaet und Familie. Paris, Alcan, 1936.

—— The Fear of Freedom. London, The International Library of Sociology and Social Reconstruction. Kegan Paul, 1942.

—— Zur Psychologie des Verbrechers und der strafenden Gesellschaft. *Im. XVII.*

GARMA, A. Psychologie des Selbstmordes. *Im. XXIII.*

GINSBERG, M. A Symposium on the Psychology of Peace and War. British Journal of Medical Psychology, xiv.

GINSBERG, M. Psychology and Sociology. In: Further Papers on the Social Sciences: Their Relations in Theory and Teaching, ed. by J. E. Dugdale. Le Play House Press, London, 35 Gordon Square, 1937.

GLOVER, E. Psychology and the Social Sciences. In: Further Papers on the Social Sciences: Their Relations in Theory and Teaching, ed. by J. E. Dugdale. London, Le Play House Press, 35 Gordon Square, 1937.

—— Das Institut zur wissenschaftlichen Behandlung der Kriminalitaet in London. *Psa. Bew. V.*

—— Fear and Courage. Middlesex Harmondsworth, Penguin Books, 1940.

—— Notes on the Psychological Effects of War Conditions on the Civilian Population. *Int. J. Psa. XXII, XXIII.*

—— Symposium on the Psychology of War and Peace. British Journal of Medical Psychology, vol. xiv, 1934.

—— The Danger of Being Human. London, George Allen and Unwin, Ltd., 1936.

—— Ueber die durch den Krieg verursachten Aenderungen in unserer psychischen Oekonomie. *Im. XXV.*

—— War, Sadism, and Pacifism. London, George Allen and Unwin, Ltd., 1933.

GLOVER, J. (with others). Social Aspects of Psychoanalysis. London, Williams and Norgate, 1924.

GORER, G. Theories of Japanese Culture. Transactions, N.Y. Acad. of Sci., 1943, v. 106–124.

—— The Special Case of Japan. Pub. Opinion Quarterly, vii, 1943.

GRABER, H. Unterwuerfigkeit. *Zeit. f. psa. Päd. II.*

HARTMANN, H. Psychoanalysis and Sociology in Lorand. Ed.: Psychoanalysis To-day, 1944, 326–341.

—— and KRIS, E. The Genetic Approach to Psychoanalysis.

—— —— The Psychoanalytic Study of the Child, vol. i, 1945.

HOLLOMAN, L. L. On the Supremacy of the Negro Athlete in White Competition. *Psa. Rev. XXX.*

HORNEY, K. The Neurotic Personality of Our Time. New York, Norton; London, Kegan Paul, 1937.

—— Culture and Neurosis. American Sociological Review, vol. 1936.

—— New Ways in Psychoanalysis. New York, 1933.

ISAACS, S. Social Development in Young Children. London, Routledge, 1933.

JONES, E. Die englische "Schicklichkeit". *Alm. 1930.*

—— Essays in Applied Psychoanalysis: P. 360, War and Individual Psychology; P. 381, War and Sublimation; P. 398, The Island of Ireland: A Psychological Contribution to Political Psychology. London, The International Psychoanalytical Press, 1923.

—— Evolution and Revolution. *Int. J. Psa. XXII.*

—— How Can Civilization be Saved? *Int. J. Psa. XXIV.*

—— On the Nightmare. London, The Hogarth Press and the Institute of Psychoanalysis, 1931.

JONES, E. Psychoanalyse und Anthropologie. *Int. J. Psa. X.*
—— Psychoanalyse und Religion. Das Psychoanalytische Volksbuch, p. 654. Bern, Verlag Hans Huber, 1939.
—— Psychoanalysis and the Psychology of Religion. In Psychoanalysis To-day, p. 323. New York, Covici-Friede, Pbrs., 1933.
—— The Individual and Society. Sociological Review, xxvii.
—— The Psychology of Constitutional Monarchy. New Statesman and Nation. 1st February, 1936.
—— Zur Psychoanalyse der Christlichen Religion. Wien, Internationaler Psychoanalytischer Verlag, 1928.
—— (with others). Social Aspects of Psychoanalysis. London, Williams and Norgate, 1924.
KARDINER, A. The Individual and his Society. The Psychodynamism of Social Organization. New York, Columbia University Press, 1939.
—— in collaboration with R. LINTON, CORA DU BOIS, and J. WEST. The Psychological Frontiers of Society. New York, Columbia University Press, 1945.
KELBEN, H. Der Begriff des Staates und die Sozialpsychologie. *Im. VIII.*
—— Der Staatsbegriff in der Psychoanalyse. *Alm. 1927.*
—— The Conception of the State and Social Psychology. *Int. J. Psa. V.*
KLUCKHORN, C., and MOWRER, O. Dynamic Theory of Personality. In : Personality and the Behaviour Disorders. New York, 1944, Ronald Press Co.
KOHN, E. Die Psychoanalyse in den Gesellschaftswissenschaften. Das Psychoanalitische Volksbuch, p. 573. Bern, Verlag Hans Huber, 1939.
KRIS, E. Some Problems of War Propaganda, a note on Propaganda Old and New. *Psa. Quart. XII, 1943.*
—— The " Danger of Propaganda ". American Imago, ii, 1941.
—— Danger and Morale. The Am. Journal of Orthopsychiatry, 1944, xiv.
—— The Covenant of the Gangsters. The Journ. of Criminal Psychopathiology, iv, 1943.
—— Problem der Aesthik, Intern. Zeitschrift fuer Psychoanalyse und Imago, xxvi, 1940.
—— Zur Psychologie der aelteren Biographik. *Im. XXI, 1935.*
—— and GOMBRICH, E. The Principles of Caricature. British Journ. of Medical Psychology, xvii, 1938.
KROEBER, A. Totem and Taboo in Retrospect. Amer. Journ. Sociol., 45, 1939.
LANDAUER, K. Das Strafvollzugsgesetz. *Psa. Bew. II.*
LASSWELL, H. D. Das Prinzip des dreifachen Apells : Ein psychoanalytischer Beitrag zur Sozialwissenschaft. *Alm. 1936* ; and The American Journal of Sociology, xxxvii, No. 4, 1932.
—— Psychoanalyse und Sozioanalyse. *Jm. XIX.*
—— Psychopathology and Politics. Chicago, University of Chicago Press, 1930.

LASSWELL, H. D. What Psychiatrists and Political Scientists can Learn from One Another. Psychiatry : A Journal of the Biology and Pathology of Interpersonal Relationships, vol. 1932.
—— Selected References of Social Psychiatry. American Journal of Sociology, vol. 1937.
—— World Politics and Personal Insecurity. McGraw Hill, 1925.
—— The Contribution of Freud's Insight. Interview to the Social Sciences. Amer. Journ. of Soc., xlv, 1939, pp. 375–390.
—— Person, Personality, Group Culture, Psychiatry, vol. 2, pp. 533–561 (1939).
LEVY, D. Sibling rivalries, studies in children of primitive groups. American Journ. of Orthopsych., 9, 1939.
LINTON, R. The Affects of Culture on Mental and Emotional Processes. Research Publication of the Association for Nervous and Mental Diseases, vol. 19, 1939, pp. 293–304.
LITTLE, G. Analytic Reflections on Mixed Marriages. *Psa. Rev. XXIX.*
LORENZ, H. Der politische Mythos. *Jm. VI.*
LOW, B. (with others). Social Aspects of Psychoanalysis. London, Williams and Norgate, 1929.
LÖWENFELD, H. Some Aspects of a Compulsion Neurosis in a Changing Civilization. *Psa. Quart., XIII,* 1944.
MADDOX, A. Some Psychophysical Aspects of the Race Problem. *Psa. Rev. XXX.*
MALINOWSKI, B. Mutterrechtliche Familie und Oedipuskomplex. *Jm. X.*
—— Psychoanalysis and Anthropology. Nature, vol. 1923.
—— Sex and Repression in a Savage Society. London, Kegan Paul, 1927. New York, Harcourt Brace, 1927.
MANNHEIM, K. Ueber die durch den Krieg verursachten Aenderungen in unserer psychischen Oekonomie. *Jm. XXV.*
—— The Sociology of Human Valuations : The Psychological and Sociological Approach, in Further Papers on the Social Sciences : Their Relations in Theory and Teaching, ed. by J. E. Dugdale. London, Play House Press, 35 Gordon Square, 1935.
—— Ideology and Utopia : An Introduction to the Sociology of Knowledge. London, Kegan Paul, 1936 ; New York, Harcourt Brace, 1936.
—— Man and Society in an Age of Reconstruction : Studies in Modern Social Structure. Especially parts i, iii, iv, 9. London, Kegan Paul, 1940 ; New York, Harcourt Brace.
—— Diagnosis of our Time. Especially ch. v. Mass Education and Group Analysis. International Library of Sociology and Social Reconstruction. London, Kegan Paul, 1943 ; New York, Oxford University Press, 1944.
MASSERMAN, J. H. Experimental Neuroses and Group Aggression. Amer. Journ. of Orthopsychiatry, vol. 14, pp. 636–643 (1944).
MCKEEL, S. An Anthropologist's Observations on American Indian Education. Progr. Educ. 13, 1936.

MEAD, M. On the Concept of Plot in Culture. Transactions of the New York Ac. of Sci., ii, vol. 2, No. 1 (1939).
—— The Cultural Approach to Personality. Trans. of N.Y. Ac. of Sci., vol. 2, pp. 93–101 (January, 1944).
—— Keep Your Powder Dry. New York, 1942.
MEKEEL, S. H. A Psychoanalytic Approach to Culture. Journal of Social Philosophy, vol. 1937.
MENNINGER, K. A. Psychoanalytic Aspects of Suicide. *Int. J. Psa. XIV.*
MONEY-KYRLE, R. Superstition and Society. Psychoanalytical Epitomes, No. 3. The Hogarth Press and The Institute of Psychoanalysis, 1938.
—— The Meaning of Sacrifice. London, The Hogarth Press and the Institute of Psychoanalysis, 1930. International Psychoanalytic Library.
OSBORN, R. Freud and Marx. London, Gollancz, 1937.
PARSONS, T. The Problem of Controlled Institutional Change, an Essay on Applied Social Science. Psychiatry, viii, 1945.
PFISTER, J. Die menschlichen Einigungsbestrebungen im Lichte der Psychoanalyse. *Jm. XII.*
—— The Psychoanalytic Study of the Child, An Annual, vol. 1. Imago Publishing Co., 1945.
PRUDHOMME, CH. The Problem of Suicide in the American Negro. *Psa. Rev. XXV.*
PRYNS HOPKINS. Father or Sons? A Study in Social Psychology. London, Kegan Paul, Trench, Trubner and Co., Ltd., 1927.
—— The Psychology of Social Movements. London, George Allen and Unwin, 1938.
RANK, O., and SACHS, H. Die Bedeutung der Psychoanalyse fuer die Geisteswissenschaften. Wiesbaden, Verlag von J. F. Bergmann, 1913.
—— The significance of psychoanalysis for the mental sciences. *R.A. II, III.*
REDL, F. Der Mechanismus der Strafwirkung. *Zeit. f. psa. Päd. IX.*
—— Group Emotion and Leadership. Psychiatry, vol. 5, pp. 573–596 (1942).
—— The Psychology of Gang Formation and the Treatment of Juvenile Delinquents. In: The Psychoanalytic Study of the Child, vol. 1 (1945).
REICH, W. Die Dialektik im Seelischen. *Alm. 1930.*
—— Die Spaltung der Geschlechtlichkeit und ihre Folgen fuer Ehe und Gesellschaft. *Alm. 1928.*
—— Die Stellung der Psychoanalyse in der Sowjet Union. *Psa. Bew. I.*
—— Discussion on the Need for Punishment and the Neurotic Process. *Int. J. Psa. IX.*
—— Geschlechtsreife, Enthaltsamkeit, Ehemoral: Eine Kritik der Buergerlichen Sexualreform. Wien, Muensterverlag.
—— Massenpsychologie des Faschismus. Kopenhagen, Verlag fuer Sexualpolitik, 1933.
REIK, TH. Der Eigene und der Fremde Gott. Wien, Internationaler Psychoanalytischer Verlag, 1923.

REIK, TH. Der Selbstverrat des Moerders. *Alm. 1933.*
—— Dogma und Zwangsidee. Wien, Internationaler Psychoanalytischer Verlag, 1927.
—— Gestaendniszwang und Strafbeduerfnis. Wien, Psychoanalytische Bibliothek, xviii, 1923.
—— Psychoanalyse und Mythes. *Zeit. f. psa. Päd. I.*
—— Psychoanalytische Strafrechstheorie. *Alm. 1926.*
—— Ritual. London, The Hogarth Press and The Institute of Psychoanalysis, 1931.
—— The Science of Religion [with bibliography], 1909–1919. *Int. J. Psa. II.*
—— The Unknown Murderer. The International Psychoanalytical Library. London, The Hogarth Press and the Institute of Psychoanalysis, 1936.
RICKMANN, J. Index Psycho-Analyticus, 1893–1926. London, The Hogarth Press and The Institute of Psychoanalysis, 1928.
—— Symposium on the Psychology of War and Peace. British Journal of Medical Psychology, vol. xiv, 1934.
ROHEIM, G. Animism and Religion. *Psa. Quart. I.*
—— Die Psychoanalytische Deutung des Kulturbegriffes. *Jm. XXVI.*
—— Die Voelkerpsychologie und die Psychologie der Voelker. *Jm. XII.*
—— La Psychologie Raciale et les Origines du Capitalisme chez les Primitifs. *Rev. Fr. de Psa. III.*
—— Primitive High Gods. *Psa. Quart. III.*
—— Psychoanalysis and Anthropology. In : Psychoanalysis To-day, p. 307. New York, Covici-Friede, Pbrs., 1933.
—— Psychoanalysis of Primitive Cultural Types. *Int. J. Psa. XIII.*
—— The Evolution of Culture. *Int. J. Psa. XV.*
—— The Garden of Eden. *Psa. Rev. XXVII.*
—— The Origin and Function of Culture. *Psa. Rev. XXIX.*
—— The Psychoanalytic Interpretation of Culture. *Int. J. Psa. XXII.*
—— The Riddle of the Sphynx. London, The Hogarth Press and the Institute of Psychoanalysis, 1934.
SACHS, H., and RANK, O. Die Bedeutung der Psychoanalyse fuer die Geisteswissenschaften. Wiesbaden, Verlag, von J. F. Bergmann, 1913.
—— The Significance of Psychoanalysis for the Mental Sciences. *Psa. Rev. II, III.*
SACHS, H. Gibt es eine Todesstrafe ? *Psa. Bew. II.*
—— The Delay of the Machine Age. *Psa. Quart. II.*
—— The Creative Unconscious, Cambridge, Sci.-Art., 1942.
ST. LINCOLN, J. The Dream in Primitive Cultures. London, The Cresset Press (1935).
SCHILDER, P. Cultural Patterns and Constructive Psychology. *Psa. Rev. XXVII.*
—— Psychoanalyse und Recht. Wiener Medizinische Wochenschrift, xxviii, Wien, 1929.
—— Psychoanalysis and Criminology. In : Psychoanalysis To-day, p. 349. New York, Covici-Friede, Pbrs., 1933.
—— Psychoanalysis of Economics. *Psa. Rev. XXVII.*

SCHILDER, P. The Analysis of Ideologies as a Psycho-therapeutic Method, especially in Group Treatment. American Journal of Psychiatry, vol. 1936.

—— Introductory Remarks on Groups. Journal of Social Psychology, vol. 1941.

—— The Relationship Between Social and Personal Disorganization. Amer. Journ. of Soc., vol. 42 (1936, 1937), 832–9.

—— Goals and Desires of Man (New York, 1942).

SEARS, R. A Survey of Objective Studies of Psychoanalytic Concepts. New York, 1943. Social Science Research Council.

SELIGMAN, C. G. Anthropology and Psychology. Journal of the Royal Anthr. Institute, liv, 13–46, 1924.

—— The Unconscious in Relation to Anthropology. Brit. Journ. Psychology, xviii, 1928, p. 373.

—— Japanese Temperament and Character. Trans. Jap. Soc. London, 28, 1931.

SELIGMAN, BRENDA. The Incest Barrier : Its Role in Social Organization. British Journ, of Psychology, xxii, pp. 250–276, 1932.

SCHMIEDEBERG, M. Erziehung und Gesellschaftsordnung. *Jm. XVIII.*

—— Zur Verstaendnis massenpsychologischer Erscheinungen. *Jm. XXI.*

SHARPE, E. (with others). Social Aspects of Psychoanalysis. London, Williams and Norgate, 1924.

STAUB, H. Psychoanalyse und Strafrecht. *Im. XVII.*

—— Psychoanalyse und Strafrecht. Das Psychoanalytische Volksburch, p. 583. Bern, Verlag Hans Huber, 1939.

—— Zum Kampf um die Todesstrafe. *Psa. Bew. III.*

STAUB, H., and ALEXANDER, F. Der Kampf ums Recht. *Psa. Bew. I.*

—— The Criminal, the Judge, and the Public. New York, The Macmillan Company, 1931.

SMITH, L. Aaron Burr. *Psa. Quart.*, vol. 12, pp. 67–99, 1943.

STERBY, R. Der orale Ursprung des Neides. *Zeit. f. psa. Päd. III.*

STORFER, J. Soziologie ohne Psychoanalyse. *Psa. Bew. II.*

" STRAFEN." Symposium of Aichhorn, Bernfeld, Weiss, Hitschmann Bohm, Yates, Schmiedeberg, Tamm, Pipal, Mannheim. *P.V.*

SYZ, H. The Social Neurosis. American Journal of Sociology, vol. 1937.

TOMASIC, D. Personality Development in the Zadruga Society. Psychiatry, vol. 5, pp. 229–261 (1942).

—— The Yearbook of Psychoanalysis. Imago Publishing Co., 1945.

WAELDER, R. Aetiologie und Verlauf der Massenpsychosen. Mit einem Soziologischen Anhang ueber die geschichtliche Situation der Gegenwart. *Jm. XXI.*

—— Die Bedeutung des Werkes Sigmund Freud's fuer die Sozial- und Rechtswissenschaften. *Alm. 1937.*

—— Die Psychoanalyse im Lebensgefuehl des modernen Menschen. *Alm. 1929.*

WHITE, W. A. Some Suggestions Regarding Practical Contacts between Sociology and Psychoanalysis. Publications of the American Sociological Society, vol. 1920.

WILLIAMS, F. E. Russia, Youth, and the Present Day World. New York, Farrar and Rinehart, 1934.
WITTELS, F. Das Sakrament der Ehe. *Alm. 1928.*
—— Die Welt Ohne Zuchthaus. Stuttgart, Hipokrates Verlag, 1928.
—— Politischer Radikalismus. *Psa. Bew. III.*
—— The Super-Ego in our Judgements of Sex. *Int. J. Psa. XIV.*
ZILBORG, G. Mind, Medicine, and Man. New York, Harcourt Brace, 1943.

INDEX OF NAMES

INDEX OF SUBJECTS

For Product Safety Concerns and Information please contact our EU representative GPSR@taylorandfrancis.com
Taylor & Francis Verlag GmbH, Kaufingerstraße 24, 80331 München, Germany

www.ingramcontent.com/pod-product-compliance
Ingram Content Group UK Ltd.
Pitfield, Milton Keynes, MK11 3LW, UK
UKHW022109190926
475702UK00013B/1338
9780415605878